CONTENTS

Copyright
Dedication
Introduction
The Five Tool Fundraiser   1
The Successful Solicitor   3
The Five Tool Fundraiser   21
The Beloved Staff Manager   23
The Five Tool Fundraiser   43
The Trusted CEO and Executive Team Partner   45
The Five Tool Fundraiser   63
The Effective Volunteer Manager   65
The Five Tool Fundraiser   93
The Thought Leader and Strategist   95
The Journey is the Destination   123
About The Author   127
About The Author   129
Praise For Author   133
Books By This Author   139

Copyright © 2023 The Five Tool Fundraiser

All rights reserved

The characters and events portrayed in this book are fictitious. Any similarity to real persons, living or dead, is coincidental and not intended by the author.

No part of this book may be reproduced, or stored in a retrieval system, or transmitted in any form or by any means, electronic, mechanical, photocopying, recording, or otherwise, without express written permission of the publisher.

ISBN-13: 9798861548410

Cover design by Jay Toffoli
Library of Congress Control Number: 2018675309
Printed in the United States of America

The Five Tool Fundraiser

The complete guide to fundraising and leadership mastery

Christopher Looney and
Claudia Looney, FAHP, ACFRE

This book is dedicated to every mission-minded fundraiser that has sought to become a stronger development professional and desired to create a better world. The best fundraisers are often unsung heroes. They are rainmakers, change agents, activators, and catalysts and their impact is beyond measure. Despite this, we often fail to recognize their work or properly acknowledge their contributions. As the authors of The Five Tool Fundraiser, we would like to show our appreciation and honor your talents.

INTRODUCTION

Baseball fans will know the term "Five Tool Baseball Player" and can probably name a few of their favorite five tool players. Willie Mays is one of the greatest baseball players that ever lived and one of my all-time favorite players. He was to some a perfect player. In his career, Willie Mays hit 660 home runs, had 12 gold gloves, 24 All-Star game appearances, had a lifetime batting average over .300, nearly 3,300 hits, 2,000 RBI, and 340 stolen bases. For those of you that don't know baseball, these are beyond impressive career statistics. Willie Mays is the quintessential five tool baseball player because he could: 1) Hit for average; 2) Hit for power; 3) Had speed; 4) Had a great throwing arm; and 5) Was very strong defensively.

Why is this relevant to us? Let us tell you why through a short story. Several years ago, the two of us were in Vancouver for the AFP International Conference. During that event, Claudia, a 50+-year fundraising veteran and mentor to many, received the AFP Fundraising Professional of the Year Award. As Chris was listening to Claudia's career achievements and thinking about the development skills that she possesses, it struck Chris as a baseball fan that if she was a baseball player, she would certainly be a Hall of Famer and would be considered a five tool player because she is good at every part of fundraising. Chris' consultant brain began to work on the idea, and he was soon spending my long drives from client to client thinking about the characteristics of the very best development professionals in our industry.

The concept of the Five Tool Fundraiser was born. Many years later, we – mother and son – collaborated to write this book, which we hope is a help to all fundraisers committed to the development profession and to advancing their capabilities forward toward achieving their true professional potential.

What is The Five Tool Fundraiser ™? The Five Tool Fundraiser ™ is a tested and proven framework for understanding the characteristics of the best and most successful development professionals in the nonprofit and fundraising industries and provides a more thoughtful and strategic approach to the work of the development professional.

We recognize and admit that there are literally hundreds of qualities and characteristics that define the best fundraisers I know. However, when we grouped them all together under overarching themes, we were able to see five characteristics or traits shared among the best of the best in our business, the fundraising Hall of Famers. And so, it was then that The Five Tool Fundraiser ™ concept was born. As we've explored this framework over the years, we continue to learn more about how to understand and apply it every day.

The five tools, as we've thought through them, are as follows:

1. The Successful Solicitor
2. The Beloved Staff Manager
3. The Trusted CEO and Executive Team Partner
4. The Effective Volunteer Support System
5. The Thought Leader and Strategist

Throughout this book we will go into more detail about each of these qualities, drilling into the most significant actions and characteristics that define greatness. The book will also provide specific examples of success by sharing real-life scenarios. And we attempt to reinforce the learning with a particularly meaningful quote.

Before we jump into the five tools, let me please briefly explain why we believe this subject is a relevant concept and framework for us and why it matters.

It's important for all of us - our organizations, bosses, staff, board members, volunteers, and donors - to understand that the best development professionals are not merely good salespeople. It takes more than just the ability to sell or close gifts to succeed in our business.

The successful development professional works in a complex environment and while soliciting can be very important to the role, other key roles and responsibilities of fundraisers are far too often overlooked. We don't often appreciate, for example, how the best fundraisers can bring together a large group of people, help them build consensus, and then march them forward toward a common goal.

People that aren't fundraisers don't understand the complexities of demands of our work. In what profession, for example, can you find yourself briefing your CEO for a request at 8 in the morning, interviewing a prospective staff member at 9, running a staff meeting at 10, making calls and sending emails at 11, meeting with a prospective donor at noon, preparing a proposal at 2, making more donors calls at 3, meeting with a prospective board member at 4pm, attending a special event at 6pm and then doing paperwork, thank you letters, all those things later that same night. That's the typical Monday.

The Five Tool Fundraiser is a good framework to help us understand our weaknesses or limitations. Why would this be helpful? How else can we grow professionally in those areas or staff up around those weaknesses? The classic example, of course, is the great solicitor who has challenges managing staff. Or it could be the other way around. The great manager that can't raise a dollar if their life depended on it.

We believe this information is helpful for hiring managers or members of hiring committees that don't know what qualities to look for in the position or positions they are trying to fill. Given the realities of our business, we really need to ask ourselves a serious question. Could this information help reduce the staff turnover that is so common in our industry? We believe so.

As two people who care deeply about our profession, we'd like to help advance people's understanding about it.

Throughout this book, the reader will be introduced to the

THE FIVE TOOL FUNDRAISER

Part I

five "tools" and within each of the tools there will be a variety of sub headers. You will find these to be roles, tasks, traits, characteristics, and actions. We understand that each of them can be interpreted in many ways.

To provide more clarity around each of the tools and sub heads, we share real-world examples through the lens of different fundraisers, sectors, and institutions. This method of storytelling we hope will leave the reader more engaged, knowledgeable, and entertained.

We are so excited to share more with you so let's not waste time and get into the five tools. Enjoy!

THE SUCCESSFUL SOLICITOR

The Successful Solicitor

A successful solicitor raises money. He or she is a rainmaker. Where others have difficulty translating their efforts with prospective donors and their pipeline or database of prospects into dollars through the door, the successful solicitor knows how to develop relationships and close gifts. The successful solicitor raises the dollars. How do you explain the challenges for some and the relative ease with which others seem to succeed in the task of raising money? There are qualities that the successful solicitor possesses that help explain this capability and result. You can't point to just one trait or characteristic. Often, it's multiple characteristics working together harmoniously. This chapter attempts to break down these necessary ingredients that distinguish the best of the best among successful solicitors.

Mission-Driven and Passionate
Let's start with the reality that the best solicitors are true believers in the cause. They are passionate about the mission of the organization (whether curing childhood cancer or protecting the rights of immigrants and everything in between). They connect the advancement of the organization – growing or sustaining programs - to the funding required from philanthropy. As a result, these fundraisers have a purpose for the work, and it drives them to do even more than they normally would under other circumstances. It's not merely a job...it's a calling.

What are your passions? Are you currently working within an area that connects to those passions? If not, consider a long-term pathway that would allow you to gain necessary and helpful experience but ultimate culminate in the position and organization of your dreams.

After college graduation, Jane went to work for her alma mater raising money in the annual fund office. She spent the next several years learning the fundraising trade and absorbed the best practices of development. She advanced to the ranks of Assistant Vice President of Major Gifts. Making a good living but not passionate about the cause, Jane jumped to a position as a front-line fundraiser for a national organization raising money to find treatments and cures for childhood cancer. Though the salary is a bit lower than it was at the university, Jane is much happier and more fulfilled now in her new role and sees herself connected to the mission and confident that she has found a new home where she can settle in and do great work for many more years.

"Every person above the ordinary has a certain mission that they are called to fulfill." - Johann Wolfgang von Goethe

Strong Institutional Knowledge

An organization's supporters are very often curious and like to know details about the organization you serve. These questions often dig far below the surface and require the fundraiser to have a substantial reservoir of information about the organization. Demonstrating that you know key details about the program, about the vision for the future of the organization, about the lives of individuals that have been served and positively impacted, about the balance sheet, size of the endowment, and much more, all contribute to the strength of your ability to communicate the value proposition of your organization to those wanting to support you.

When Dave began working for his new nonprofit, a social service provider, he quickly recognized that he didn't know enough about the various programs offered by the nonprofit. The areas that Dave wanted to know more about included the services offered, the numbers of individuals served, the people who ran those programs, the impact of those programs, and the needs of those programs that could be funded through philanthropy. From day one, Dave made it a point to schedule meetings with the leaders of each of the programs with four questions plus dozens of questions that came up during the conversation.

During his onboarding meetings, his questions were these: Could you tell me about your history with our organization? What are the strengths of our organization and, what are the strengths in your area? What are the opportunities for new and expanded programs and services? How do you want to partner with me to help raise funds to make your goals and aspirations a reality?

Before his conversation with each person, Dave studied the available materials developed which included proposals. In addition, he began to collect stories from successful program participants. Dave was focused and thorough and became an expert on the organization. Soon many sought his knowledge and understanding not just on philanthropic matters but in all matters connected to the organization.

"I have no particular talent. I am merely inquisitive." - Albert Einstein

<u>Relationship-Builder</u>
It must be hard for someone that doesn't enjoy the company of others to be a successful fundraiser. I'm not saying it's impossible to overcome this deficiency. I'm familiar with individuals that turn on the charm when

Dave has learned through the years not to be surprised about anything. Expecting one person at a meeting and five show up...no problem. Meeting with a prospective donor about a possible board role and they only want to talk about how much they dislike the CEO...no problem. Dave has become unflappable even in the face of extreme circumstances. He listens well and asks questions to learn more. He genuinely cares about other people. Dave is an extraordinary listener and adapts wonderfully to any circumstance. He remains understanding through it all and always tries his best to focus on strategies that move the relationship forward productively.

"I've learned that people will forget what you said, people will forget what you did, but people will never forget how you made them feel." — Maya Angelou

Expert Communicator

Communication comes in many forms these days. The best fundraisers have mastered written and verbal modes of communication. On the written side, we often see fundraisers producing strategy memos, business plans, general correspondence, proposals, and thousands of additional fundraising related items. On the verbal side, there are no fewer items. We often see presentations in large groups and small groups and a lot of one-on-one work including staff meetings, donor meetings, board presentations as well as the all-important one-on-one meetings with prospects and donors.

Being a strong and competent communicator is non-negotiable.

In fundraising, there is also the requirement for the best

development professionals to be expert at telling a great story. Storytelling is an essential strength of the best solicitors. What does it mean to be a great storyteller?

A good storyteller paints a picture with their words and uses descriptive language to create images that help the listener visualize the story. A good storyteller knows how to pace their stories, knowing when to speed the story up and slow it down, and uses suspense to keep the listener engaged. A good storyteller knows their audience, tailors the story to them, and shares relevant stories. Importantly, the effective solicitor can connect their great stories to actions they want the audience to take.

Judy wasn't always a great storyteller. Then one day she realized that she didn't need to create the stories but instead retell great stories effectively. Judy collected a handful of great stories from clients served by the organization that demonstrated the impact of the organization and was able to share those stories with passion and inspiration. And though the stories were repeated often, the four or five stories that Judy constantly used were ultimately key in moving thousands of people over the years to become donors.

One of Judy's favorite stories involves a patient family and their harrowing tale. As she tells it, "Imagine that you are on your 30-mile drive home from work. Your husband is in the downstairs kitchen making dinner, while your two little girls are playing upstairs in their second-floor bedroom apartment. It's a hot day so the window is open with a screen covering the opening. The girls, ages 3 and 5, are sitting on the windowsill, holding hands, and jumping from the window's edge to the bed. One, two, three they yell with glee and jump to the bed from the window. On their third try, they began rocking back and forth and fall back against the screen, which gives way, and they fall from the 2nd story window to the cement sidewalk below. Dad rushes outside to find your little girls not moving. He makes a frantic call to 911. The girls are soon on board a helicopter to the children's hospital, where their lives are saved. They spend three months in the hospital, during which time they receive expert physical therapy, occupational therapy, and speech therapy in addition to multiple orthopedic surgeries. In the end, the girls, now ages 6 and 8, are in dance classes and learning how to be ballerinas. This is just one example of thousands of why our children's hospital is so critical and needs your support."

"The most amazing thing for me is that every single person who sees a movie, not necessarily one of my movies, brings a whole set of unique experiences, but through careful manipulation and good storytelling, you can get everybody to clap at the same. time, to hopefully laugh at the same time, and to be afraid at the same time." - Steven Spielberg

Asks for Support
Our experience is that many fundraisers don't make "real" asks. If they do, it's rare. Instead, most fundraisers allow gifts to come in "over the transom," which means the gifts come into an organization without a specific or intentional request. And yes, even now and then, "a blind squirrel finds a nut." No one should ever complain about gifts coming in over the transom. But there is money absolutely left on the table when fundraisers don't proactively pursue and ask their potential funders for support and instead allow their potential funders to make their own decisions.

We believe fear is what prevents most fundraisers from

making the ask. The fear of rejection. The fear of ruining the relationship. The fear of saying the wrong thing. The fear of failure. The fear of the unknown. All these fears and more can creep into the mind of fundraisers and prevent them from doing the one thing that is generally required to result in success.

Activity creates results and the right activity creates the right results. If there is something that prevents the fundraiser from making asks, it's a problem.

The best fundraisers we know don't have that fear or at least they don't let it get in their way. If fundraising is in your DNA, it comes as second nature to you. Approaching asks without hesitation or reservation demonstrates that you are focused on advancing the organization's mission. It's not about you personally. You are not raising money for yourself. You are helping another person accomplish something very important with their charitable investments. As Hank Rosso points out, "fundraising is the gentle art of teaching the joy of giving."

The best fundraisers know when it is the right time and the right ask to be making of the right prospective donor. Either the fundraiser has it in their DNA or they know how to push their fears aside and rise to the occasion to be able to make the ask and do it in such a way that it feels comfortable and natural for the person being asked. They know that often the ask must be a specific amount, direct, and not just a hint or suggestion. Good fundraisers also know that having a good relationship with the prospective donor enhances their comfort level in making "the ask."

Many will argue that if the cultivation process has been conducted properly, the ask is an easy and natural needed, even though it is not as natural as you might hope. My father, a very successful development professional and even more successful fundraising consultant, embodies the ability to succeed by flipping the switch on his own personality (turning on the charm button) when necessary and appropriate. That's a huge talent! When activated, my father was comfortable and happy. But I can tell you that it was not natural. It's far easier when that charm is part of your DNA.

Even more than spending time with people, it is necessary and helpful to build trusting and mutually beneficial relationships intentionally and authentically with all types of individuals over time. This includes strong relationships with donors, board members, volunteers, prospective donors, and staff. Meaningful engagements and sustained engagements over time are the pathways to success.

Examples of successful relationship-building tactics include proactively engaging through meals, phone calls, text, and notes; caring about the things the other person cares about especially including their children and grandchildren; celebrating key events in their life with them like birthdays and anniversaries and dates connected with their engagement in the organization; being a resource and available to them when they have a need a helping hand; and so much more.

Over the years, Stella has developed a contact system for the 200 prospective donors in her portfolio. She knows the birthdays of each of the family members of these prospective donors and this birthday list numbers nearly 1,000. Stella proactively reaches out with a happy personalized birthday message on those dates. Twice a year at a minimum she gets together for an update lunch or coffee and shares meaningful stories about the organization and the clients served, always maintaining client confidentiality. She extends invites regularly to events she knows the prospective donor will appreciate and at least once a year there is a discussion focused on the impact and results of the gifts provided by the donor and either an outright request or discussion about goals and possible future support.

"Do what you can to show you care about other people, and you will make our world a better place." - Rosalynn Carter

<u>Knows Audience and Empathizes</u>
The best fundraisers I know are experts at understanding relationship dynamics, adjusting approaches and language to the unique audiences they confront. Like a chameleon, the best fundraisers adapt to their surroundings as if by second nature. They know their audience and understand what needs to be said and how strongly or subdued the conversation needs to be handled.

If you are a successful solicitor, you are likely to pick up on cues from the prospective donor well. This means you can listen and respond extremely well and understand when to push forward and when to hold back. You empathize with your audience and show authentic caring for their situation. You are credible and believable, and people feel comfortable being in your presence and opening up to you about their hopes and dreams and fears and concerns.

Many great fundraisers have been labeled as effective therapists...not because of the advice they give but for their ability to listen well and ask the right questions. This allows the donor or prospective donor to feel heard, appreciated, and then they tend to open up.

extension and will typically lead to an expected outcome.

It is likely that fears and inaction exist because the muscle it takes to make an ask has not yet been well enough developed. What do I mean? Nothing is easy in the beginning. You can't run a marathon after one day of training. You must log miles and repeat and repeat again and train and execute before you can build the bodily capacity to survive all 26.2 miles. It's like asking for gifts. Making one ask doesn't make you an expert and doesn't make you comfortable. Every ask you make helps build the muscle to be able to do it more effectively the next time. After 100 or 1,000 asks, you finally start realizing that the thing that was so difficult before is easier with experience. And recency is important as well. If you've let years pass since you made asks (even if they were substantial in number), there will be likely be atrophy of the fundraising muscles and certainly some rust. The only antidote is to ask and ask frequently.

Sometime being an effective solicitor means asking when the CEO, a board member, or a volunteer can't find the words to ask for a gift from the prospective donor. We've personally been put in that awkward position many times when we quickly recognize the responsibility to get the ask out rests on our shoulders. In those situations, if you're not prepared to make the ask yourself, the window might close forever. If not you, who? If not now, when?

Dave was recently in a meeting with his Executive Director and a prospective donor. The prospective donor had not yet supported the organization financially but is considered by many to be a strong board member candidate. Dave and his CEO know that this individual cares deeply about the organization's mission and is known to be a proven philanthropist to other causes. The goal of the meeting was to ask the individual for a first-ever gift to support a program that Dave and the CEO thought would be of interest to him. And they also wanted to explore the possibility of future board leadership. Dave and the CEO had met prior to the meeting to review the written strategy - the script and the details of the ask that Dave had expertly prepared. They prepared backwards and forwards for the meeting, even with role-playing. The roles were clearly defined and practiced. The CEO was to make the ask for the gift and leadership consideration. When the time came to make those requests, the CEO froze like a deer in headlights. Like a pro, Dave stepped in and without missing a beat, made the ask for financial support and board leadership successfully. The new donor wasn't even aware of the CEO's failure. Mission accomplished.

"The brave man is not he who does not feel afraid, but he who conquers that fear."
--Nelson Mandela

Goal-Oriented and Metrics-Focused

The most effective solicitors are not afraid to be evaluated. Rather, they are performance-based and motivated to achieve. They desire the capacity to measure success and impact – especially their own - and appreciate a scorecard. They want to know their goals and what success looks like. It's often the accountability created by goals and metrics, that when combined with the drive of an achiever, creates the environment for extraordinary productivity.

In baseball, players are evaluated constantly through statistics. Players are measured by their batting average, OPS, ERA, and dozens of other interesting calculations. As the front office of the MLB teams will tell you, the numbers don't lie. The same is true in fundraising. Amount raised, proposals submitted, meaningful calls made, solicitation meetings completed, and so much more. Measurements of activity and measurements of results can and should be acceptable and embraced.

Success allows the effective solicitor to make the strong case for promotions and compensation increases. The effective solicitor enjoys competition and often competes and compares personal achievements – publicly or privately - with others in the organization, or with peers at aspirational peer organizations.

Many might perceive this as too competitive, cutthroat, or antithetical to the culture of a nonprofit institution. It's not an ugliness to be compared and measured. It's an extension of the competition that has generally filled their life from youth sports to college musical competitions and everything in between. And high performing development professionals and CEOs know it's necessary to measure success. The high performing development professionals that push themselves to higher and higher activity and fundraising production levels are very often the ones that drive a significant percentage of an organization's annual revenues and become irreplaceable to an organization's success.

Debra, a fundraiser at a highly regarded university, has always been a competitive person. Her college basketball coach described her as persistent and focused. She always practiced hard and extra. Now, as a member of the major gifts team at a large university, Debra appreciates coming into each year with a very clear set of objectives to meet for the coming fiscal year. The new, higher goal isn't scary to Debra. She embraces that goal and has developed action goals for herself in terms of portfolio size, contacts and meetings per week, and proposals submitted monthly that are necessary for her to achieve her goals. She actually has set stretch goals for herself to exceed the expectations. Debra knows that achieving her goals will go a long way toward helping the university succeed in its mission.

The university appreciates the work that Debra does and pays her a competitive salary through a combination of base salary and achievement bonuses. It is a "win-win" scenario. By doing well, Debra is compensated appropriately, and she is earning enough that over time, she will be able to make a down payment on a new home and accomplish her own personal financial goals.

"Never quit. It is the easiest cop-out in the world. Set a goal and don't quit until you attain it. When you do attain it, set another goal, and don't quit until you reach it. Never quit." – Bear Bryant

<u>Effective Time Management and Prioritization</u>
Effective solicitors are focused. In a world where development professionals are expected to do so much, there are countless activities that pull fundraisers away from the actual work of raising money. The most effective fundraisers expertly manage their time so that they don't fall into traps of inactivity. They protect their time for those activities that produce revenue.

Think of all the emails, calls, and meetings that take up time from the day. The best fundraisers in the world aren't immune. If anything, these individuals are bombarded more than your usual fundraisers because of their success. Everyone wants a piece of their time.

The professional gatherings and leadership responsibilities, for example, like AFP or CASE or AHP or any of the other professional associations, take up quite a bit of time. Also, the best fundraisers are often responsible for staff management, and that means hiring, managing, reviewing, and other responsibilities that come with people management. There just aren't enough hours in the day and we've only scratched the surface in terms of the things that creep into the day.

The effective solicitor is not immune from distraction or the pressures that extract them away from frontline fundraising activity. Rather, they prioritize their time differently. They don't begrudge the list of tasks that keep mounting. Rather, they embrace their many tasks, spend time prioritizing the checklist, and celebrate the accomplishments of completing those tasks.

The most effective solicitors know what needs the attention first and most. They can prioritize the "to do" list. They know what is going to get the results, and they manage their precious time extremely well and carefully. They protect time each day or during each week for prospect communications, for prospect meetings, for proposal development, for strategy development, for meeting preparation, for follow up, and they even protect time for strategy development either quietly and personally or in a group think tank mode.

George learned at an early age in his professional career that if he didn't block time on his calendar each day for the work that brought in the dollars, he would fail to generate sufficient activity to guarantee his success. George made it a habit of reserving two hours each day for prospect and donor calls and communication. George also set a goal of five in person meetings a week with donors and prospects – in home visits, coffees, breakfasts, lunches, or dinners – spread over the seven days of the week. Nothing except vacation time prevented George from hitting these targets and if the time was reserved on his calendar for everyone to see, there is no question that other meetings and priorities would have easily crept in and taken over. How did George do this? Every morning he reviewed his priority list for the day and for the week. He evaluated each task and gave them a 1,2 or 3 rating. He always did the #1 things first, the #2 things next. The #3 things probably did not happen. There just wasn't time to do everything. But he always prioritized his daily and weekly donor visits and "moves" as priority #1. George planned and managed his time. He did not let the time manage him.

"Give me six hours to chop down a tree and I will spend the first four sharpening the axe". -Abraham Lincoln

Proper Planning, Execution, and Follow-Up
Successful fundraising is a complex dance. There are so many moving parts. Success takes both great choreography and capable dancers. In the dance itself, someone leads, and someone follows. It takes great teamwork to succeed. The metaphor is helpful to understanding the fundraising process.

The successful solicitor is frequently called upon to be the choreographer and the dancer both. However, it's not a solo act. Very often, the best fundraising results are achieved when a team is assembled. Fundraising has been called a team sport...not an individual one.

The best fundraisers know that positive results can be

achieved when the right solicitation team is put in front of the prospect asking for the right gift amount for the right program at the right time. To assure the proper environment is achieved, the fundraiser is asked to be the choreographer of the dance.

Despite the very significant role played by the fundraising, the best development professionals don't need glory. They are selfless members of the team, looking to create the most favorable environment for a successful outcome. Sometimes this means the fundraiser is at the forefront and other times it means the fundraiser is taking a back seat.

The successful solicitor is masterful at coordination and execution – organization, implementation, and follow up. As someone that might be driving the entire process forward, there are so many details that must come together at the right time. Nothing falls through the cracks. In thinking about the major tasks associated with planning, execution and follow up, I offer the following: setting the meeting, determining the particulars of the ask, preparing the proposal and materials, briefing the team for the meeting, making arrangements for the ask such as dinner reservations and the like, confirming everything, supporting the ask meeting to make sure everything goes off without a hitch, determining the follow-up strategy, executing the post ask thank you notes and communication, following up to close the gift. These are very standard and typical steps that the effective solicitor holds responsibility for executing successfully.

Amber has been cultivating a family for the naming gift of the business school for the last several years. Behind the scenes, Amber has been working closely with the family office representative on the particulars. Though things seem promising, the family is known to be mercurial and the connections to the university are not as strong as the ties with some of the other principal gift prospects in her portfolio. The time has arrived to bring the family onto campus for "the ask". Amber oversees every detail. The date and time have been set, invites have been issued, and the attendance and participation of the University President, Board Chair, Dean of the Business School, and Chief Advancement Officer have been confirmed. The presentation is polished, the proposal packet is prepared, the tour details and lunch menu are set, and several other fun surprises have been arranged. Where will Amber be during the meeting? Amber will be behind the scenes, on her phone coordinating and giving instructions. Is she disappointed not to be in the room? Not at all. Amber has her eye on the prize which is securing the $25 million gift for the university. Like the dance choreographer, Amber has made certain that it is time for the curtain to come up. She has checked that all the dancers are on stage at the right time and that they have practiced their moves. She has checked the lighting and the music. The fundraising "dance" is ready to begin.

"A really great talent finds its happiness in execution." -Johann Wolfgang von Goethe

THE FIVE TOOL FUNDRAISER

Part II

THE BELOVED
STAFF MANAGER

The Beloved Staff Manager

There is probably no more challenging task for the development professional than the management of staff.

Through the decades of our fundraising work, the two most consistent challenges we confronted were staff turnover and the fundraiser that was talented at raising money but terrible at managing staff. I've heard the complaint a million times. "My manager," says the fundraiser, "can't manage themselves out of a paper bag. They might be good at raising money, but they are terrible at managing me and my teammates."

It shouldn't be surprising to us that fundraisers struggle to manage staff. Most don't receive training or adequate preparation in anticipation of management responsibilities. Most managers in the fundraising field are thrown into the fire. They didn't come from management backgrounds. They didn't get MBAs. Most managers in the fundraising field aren't given these people management responsibilities because they've exhibited the characteristics of an effective manager. Rather, staff managers in fundraising are most often promoted into these roles because they have proven themselves to be effective solicitors. They have advanced into these very significant management roles because they were top producers and needed to be promoted or the organization would lose them to some other nonprofit.

Unfortunately, being an effective solicitor doesn't prepare you at all to be a good manager. While it is true that a good fundraiser is normally a people person and has a high emotional IQ. One of the biggest issues is that they are super high performers and don't have the patience for those that are not as talented and don't have the time or the skills to mentor and train those to become higher performers.

Peter Drucker, perhaps the founder of modern management, promoted the concept of the knowledge worker. The knowledge worker is perhaps the most appropriate description of the development professional. They have a set of skills, a set of knowledge that is transferable from one organization to the next. But these same individuals are also not managed best through a command-and-control kind of management style, which is how most highly successful salespeople or fundraisers approach the work. What they often fail to comprehend is that every fundraising is unique and different, and each requires a different kind of management approach. Recognizing the proper way to manage and support staff is just one of the many critically important aspects that the Five Tool Fundraiser uses in management to bring out the best in the people they manage.

On the following pages we take a deep dive into many of the extremely relevant and important elements that the best fundraiser managers incorporate into their daily practice that makes them uniquely exceptional in this realm.

<u>Hires the Best</u>
Fundraising is a team sport. Naturally, if you have a great team, you are very likely to succeed. The best development professionals are responsible for building a great team and then sustaining and growing it for the long term. Building a great team is a requirement yet is so difficult to accomplish for most. Success often starts with the hiring process.

Hiring great people is essential for the development professional. We all know that the good individuals that work in development are hard to find and hard to keep. Often, the result is constant openings on the team that need to be filled. Filling those open spots with experienced and talented professionals that will contribute to the positive culture and revenue production is no easy task. The best managers hire the best people.

There are several characteristics that are most relevant and important to consider when looking for a successful development staff person. These are the "Seven F's of Claudia Looney". The seven F's are:

1. Focus – Are they focused on the priorities, and do they demonstrate that in terms of their last position?
2. Fast - Do they manage multiple inputs at the same time effectively and can they accomplish tasks successfully with speed and accuracy?
3. Flexible - Can they change with changed circumstances, particularly with changing leadership, disappointments, and plans turned upside down?
4. Friendly - Do they have empathy for their fellow staff or for the organization's constituents and for others? Do they have the right kind of relationships with internal staff, donors and volunteers? Are they good networkers?
5. Fundamentally Sound - Did they come from another shop that does fundraising well? Have they learned well through their past experiences? Do they pay attention to details? Do they take

pride in the quality of their work?
6. Fundraising Production - Do they have evidence of successful fundraising? Have they personally closed gifts or been a key part of the team that has secured significant support? Do they know fundraising fundamental tactics? Do they understand that when all is "said and done" that their job is to raise money, not to attend meetings?
7. Fun - Are they fun to be around? Do they enjoy their work? Do they know how to celebrate fundraising successes and have fun at work?

The degree to which you can identify, hire, and retain development professionals with these qualities will directly influence your own success as a leader.

In previous leadership roles, Dan felt pressure to micromanage every situation. It was not until he arrived at his present organization and position, where the team he inherited had significant strength and capabilities, that he realized that he was limited from reaching his full potential as a fundraiser and leader in those prior roles because his teammates were too weak. Dan now prioritizes recruiting exceptionally talented and capable individuals and won't settle for anything less. He now trusts his staff. He knows they are prioritizing the right things to do first. The staff is responding fast to donor requests. They are keeping the momentum moving forward, developing good relationships throughout the organization and externally with donors and volunteers. They are using good fundraising tactics and are producing quality work that makes the organization proud. And they are raising lots of money and having fun at the same time!

"Teamwork is the ability to work together toward a common

vision. The ability to direct individual accomplishments toward organizational objectives. It is the fuel that allows common people to attain uncommon results." – Andrew Carnegie

Minimizes Turnover – Promotes Longevity
The great lament of so many leaders in the nonprofit space is that development professionals don't have longevity. I believe this is most often the result of poor compensation. Human service salaries in fundraising are comparatively weak and, in many cases, are not competitive in the marketplace. The temptation to move laterally or higher to health care or academics and earn significantly more is just too reasonable and sensible to stay at a nonprofit no matter how much you love the mission. There are true believers that stay out of principle, and passion for the mission, but the more common track is the departure after a year or eighteen months.

It's impossible to be a "great" fundraiser if you only spend a year or so with an organization. You can be effective, and you can show signs of greatness, but you can't be great. How long it will take at an institution to become a great fundraiser is debatable. It's probably at least three years to really be able to distinguish yourself as a fundraiser who is personally responsible for driving significant philanthropy into an organization.

The five tool fundraising managers reduce turnover because they are a trusted advisor, a mentor, demonstrate caring and have concern for the personal and professional growth of staff. They create a strong culture of excellence and find the delicate balance between autonomy and engagement. An effective manager utilizes helpful tactics to increase retention and longevity including bonuses and ladders for growth in title and responsibility. These are just a few of the many ways a strong staff manager successfully reduces turnover and keeps the team intact for longer than is normal at a nonprofit.

Jan stepped into an organization that had strong philanthropic growth potential but paid staff far less than other area nonprofits. Jan understood that increased investment was required but the board was surprised that half the future investment proposed was designated not to new positions but to across-the-board salary increases to bring current staff up to same level as their peers at other nonprofits. She also included an annual inflation plan that assured salary growth would keep ahead of inflation. Finally, she instituted a bonus program. All these moves focused on retention, and they worked. Development staff stayed longer. Morale improved. The fundraising productivity improved. And Jan was respected as a manager and leader, who cared for the financial well-being of her staff. Importantly, the fundraising continued to exceed its increasingly aggressive financial goals annually.

"Where the grass is greener, the water bill is bigger." -Rick Warren

<u>Driven to Help Staff Succeed</u>
The best managers are driven to see their teams succeed. This requires that managers support the individual members of the team to reach their full potential, which in the aggregate will help the unit achieve impact. To accomplish this, the manager must be available, flexible, and capable of addressing a multitude of situations and circumstances in a positive and constructive way.

Unfortunately, there are so many things that get in the way.

The patience and capabilities of managers are constantly being tested. For some, the stress of it all can be too much, and emotions will run wild if not checked. We've all seen or heard about the 'blow ups' of managers that let situational stress get the better of them. This doesn't happen to the beloved staff managers. They are too measured and thoughtful. They certainly wouldn't respond emotionally to a highly charged email or verbal exchange right away. They will let tempers wain. Unflappable is often a way to describe the best managers.

Beyond the handling of difficult situations, great managers show up when staff need help. This might be a professional or personal need. Great managers go out of their way to help position those they supervise for success. I've known managers babysit for their staff member while that staff member took an important meeting or call. I've known managers that stay late into the evening to help staff stuff envelopes and arrange table settings for a gala. I've known managers who joined meetings with donors to help model the right behavior, reviewed proposals, or just listened with sympathy as staff complained about a myriad of challenges. The great managers show up and lend a helpful hand.

Ricky believed staff annual reviews were important to evaluate job effectiveness, understand job satisfaction, and determine goals for the next year or longer. Though time consuming, reviews were an essential element to staff growth. However, Ricky knew these meetings didn't go far enough. Ricky therefore started meeting with all direct reports quarterly to be able to measure progress more actively toward goals and understand employee satisfaction. These quarterly staff check-in meetings were so effective that Ricky asked all managers to prioritize these meetings with the staff they managed. The quarterly meetings helped all staff to stay focused on the priorities and when it came time for the annual review, there were no surprises. The annual review turned into a welcome and healthy discussion about the possibilities, goals, and outcomes for the coming year. The annual review also focused on the staff member's desire for professional growth during the coming year. The result was a helpful and enjoyable discussion rather than a focus on what all that had gone wrong during the year. Any issues had already been addressed in a timely manner and the problem was instead, "in the rear-view mirror" and did not need to be revisited.

"Management is doing things right; leadership is doing the right things" -Peter Drucker

<u>Significant Care and Feeding – Understands Keys to Job Satisfaction</u>
Much has been written about the current generation of younger workers. They are different than older generations. The more resistant to adaptation and acceptance of this reality, the harder it is for a manager to be successful. The beloved manager is quick to embrace the uniqueness of a younger generation of staff members. But let's be honest, it's not the younger generation alone that provides challenges. Each individual staff member brings with them to the job a unique set of expectations and "baggage" that is laid often at the feet of a manager. The beloved manager can adapt to the special needs of each staff member, young or old, and invests heavily in their job satisfaction.

The beloved manager is not a push over. The beloved

manager is firm but fair, consistent, and balanced. The expectations are clear and the opportunity to bring forward concerns is present. The respect earned by the successful manager is the result of the significant care and feeding the manager provides. This can often mean the manager is giving the staff member opportunities to grow and gain new experiences and is taking care to provide proper work-life balance when it counts by being sensitive to personal issues. There is also the manager's ability to understand the keys to job satisfaction for the individual staff member. While some staff might be focused on title and salary growth primarily, other staff might be more motivated by mission impact and flex schedules. These are just a small number of the many ways the effective manager maintains goodwill and good performance.

Jeremy continues to lose staff. Since joining the team six months ago, ten members of the 35-member development team have turned over. With any leadership transition, some level of staff attrition is natural. Seeing a third of the staff turnover in less than a year, including some of the strongest members of the team, has raised the concerns of the CEO. Exit interviews point to a similar cause for the departures. "it's my way or the highway" with Jeremy. Those departing shared a lack of individualized attention and support. The CEO has shared with Jeremy that he needs to adjust her style or risk losing more staff and her job.

"Any fool can criticize, condemn, and complain but it takes character and self-control to be understanding and forgiving."
-Dale Carnegie

<u>Creates a Culture of Excellence</u>
As we have discussed, there is no single management style that is effective with every staff person. No matter the style

you adopt or deliver, you need to provide for all staff a nurturing environment and endeavor to constantly build a culture of excellence.

A culture of excellence means that every person in the department strives to do their best and contribute meaningfully in their roles to the success of the overall team. There are several ways for the best managers to accomplish this. One of the ways is to create a positive working environment and this leads to a strong esprit de corps where every member of the team understands that they are individually important, but the team is more important than any one person.

There is not a team in sports, nor in the workplace, that thrives consistently over time when the leader at the top is not respected. It is so important for the staff manager to be perceived as a role model and understood to be knowledgeable and understands how to move the fundraising enterprise forward successfully.

Additionally, the ability to not take credit for yourself, but instead give it freely and abundantly to others is incredibly important. To be someone who needs to constantly be celebrated and takes the credit for the success of the team, is completely inconsistent with building a culture of excellence. I've always found that the little trick of pushing praise for successes onto other staff goes a long way to fostering the proper culture within a team.

Jenny has read several books on leading teams effectively and through her conversations with her success coach, she has developed the following six strategies for creating a culture of excellence on her team. 1. Set a positive example. 2. Establish trust. 3. Remind employees of their purpose and the mission of the organization. 4. Offer your support and praise. 5. Check in with employees regularly and show care and concern for their well-being. 6. Practice active listening.

"Perfection is not attainable, but if we chase perfection we can catch excellence." - Vince Lombardi

Metrics-Focused and High but Reasonable Expectations
It's far too easy these days to eliminate or fail to use metrics as a method of evaluating the production and effectiveness of staff. There was a time not long ago when a fundraiser's production and activity was more routinely calculated. There was also a time when asking for specific gifts was more routinely practiced. We've become soft in a lot of areas as managers. The failure to set proper fundraising and activity production goals and then monitor and evaluate those on a regular basis is one of those areas that too many managers have failed to champion.

There is a school of thought among many organizations, leaders, and workers that an emphasis on numbers dehumanizes the experience of workers. Participation trophies and achievement badges should be given to all. It's giving your best effort that matters. None of this is true in fundraising where high levels of the right activity are the strongest predictor of success and what you measure gets movement. This is important so let me say it again. What you measure gets movement. If you don't measure the activity and production of your staff, your results will miss the mark.

There is also a reality that many organizations and leaders confront which is the budget available to institute the tracking systems necessary or the lack of technical expertise that prevents organizations from implementing proper evaluation tools and mechanisms. Neither of these should be excuses for the fundraising staff manager. The best, even if operating on thin budgets, will create makeshift and free solutions on excel. When the system capabilities exist but nothing is constructed to measure, track and evaluate, one can hardly blame staff even if they lack the expertise. The staff manager has the responsibility to build and implement the system using whatever resources are required to get it done. The same development shops that fail to measure activity and production are nine times out of ten the same organizations that do not require contact reports to be entered and don't look weekly at the number of meetings completed, contact reports entered, and other moves made. The best fundraising managers would never let this important opportunity to be lost.

To some, this type of hyper focus on numbers and activity might seem arcane or harsh. Regardless of appearances, it's necessary and fair. It's necessary because it provides clarity to everyone about the objectives and expectations of the job. It's fair because the best fundraising managers will have established reasonable goals for each staff position. The expectations are not unfair or unreasonable and have been carefully developed in close cooperation with those expected to meet and exceed the goals.

If you asked his team, they would all tell you that Rickey has high expectations. Interestingly, his staff would not have it any other way. The team members are now all high performers. In the beginning, the team was concerned about the time it would take to enter metrics, such as actions and next steps. Their fears were soon replaced with the joy of seeing how helpful tracking metrics and measuring outcomes were to securing gift commitments. They appreciated the scorecard and clarity about measuring performance and success. Yes, the team didn't always resonate with this approach or style, and it was hard in those early years. In fact, it was not until Rickey was able to weed out the non-producing fundraisers and replace them with success-driven development staff, did the culture of excellence begin to take hold. The team and the results have never been stronger. His fundraising team wants to be successful. They know they are successful when they proudly review their own metrics.

"Measurement is the first step that leads to control and eventually to improvement. If you can't measure something, you can't understand it. If you can't understand it, you can't control it. If you can't control it, you can't improve it." -H. James Harrington

<u>Accepts Responsibility for Staff Failures</u>
In fundraising, like baseball, you fail more than you succeed. If you're not failing, you're not really fundraising. Fundraisers don't always hear yes. Fundraisers don't bat 1,000 when they ask. The yield on asks when you aggregate all the ask activity together can be low, often hovering around 30%. At times it can be heartbreaking to lose more than you win. But the best fundraisers keep at it and know that a hall of fame fundraiser bats .300 like a hall of fame baseball hitter.

Managers, for their part, help their team understand these realities and encourage them to keep pushing and keep the activity high, as the only real predictor of success. When failures happen, and that will happen, the best managers will find ways to help up the fundraiser, engage them in discussing and learning how to improve the ask the next time. A good manager helps the staff to feel supported and less vulnerable.

Accepting responsibility for staff failures is not limited to when a donor says, "no" or "not right now" or "not at that level". Accepting responsibility for staff failures comes when the department doesn't achieve its revenue targets, when a key member of the team departs, a keynote speaker at an event doesn't show up, the room is empty for an event, or any other countless activities that would qualify as unsuccessful fundraising, or a failure. The best managers don't shift blame, they accept and share the responsibility, and sometimes it's an overshare. They don't "throw their staff under the bus" to "save their own bacon." The best managers are grown-ups, and they recognize that anything negative that occurs on the manager's watch is the responsibility of the manager.

LaShonda remembers the pain it caused her personally and other members of the development team when her manager wouldn't take ownership and responsibility for mistakes or total misses. Instead, her boss told everyone including the CEO and others, that the blame was specifically on a particular individual, who the manager identified by name. LaShonda, now a manager herself, doesn't manage her team like that at all. When staff fail to deliver appropriately in some way, LaShonda tells her staff privately that she's got their back and though the mistake was real and significant, LaShonda acknowledges that she bears some responsibility as well and together, they will fix that mistake. And most importantly, they both learn from the mistake and try never to make that mistake again.

"The price of greatness is responsibility." — Winston Churchill

Organization's Top Cheerleader

At the 2008 Beijing Olympics, Team USA's men's 4×100-meter swim relay defeated their French rivals in one of the best in-race comebacks sports has ever seen. Michael Phelps, perhaps the greatest competitive swim racer of all-time, was a natural leader of the team. But it was his teammates that helped Phelps secure the gold for the USA and for his own record books. The race is important from the lens of management in the sense that Phelps was a producer but also a manager and a cheerleader. If you look at film footage from the race, there is no person on the pool deck more rabidly cheering on his teammates than Phelps.

The same is true of the best managers in fundraising. While they are very often individual contributors, they are a valued member of a team and always a vocal cheerleader for the efforts of their teammates. They are also the first to support and celebrate the work and efforts of all the staff and leadership of their organization. The support they provide is notable in that it helps encourage and recognize those that often are the unsung heroes. But it is critical in the way that it infects and motivates others to go far beyond the normal expectations and exceed all expectations for themselves and their supervisors.

Few people know that Victor was a cheerleader in college. The experience prepared him well for leading a small team of fundraisers at a local human service provider. His cheerleading experience required more than just physical skills and strengths. Cheerleading also helped develop Victor's skills and sportsmanship. Discipline, hard work, teamwork, physical fitness, mental strength, confidence and self-esteem, community outreach, leadership, social skills, perseverance, and dedication were all leadership skills that he used and implemented in his daily encounters with his team and the leaders and staff of his organization. Important to Victor was the discovery that his cheerleading experience helped him root for the success of others and understand that the success of others reflected very positively on his own achievements. His cheerleading for his organization was heartfelt and his honesty and caring created the added benefit of being a trusted leader and one who had their back when the team was scoring wins and when it did not. Victor was a dependable advocate and a positive-thinking leader for his team and the organization.

"The most beautiful people are those who bring out the beauty in others." – Matshona Dhliwayo

Not Afraid to Have the Tough Conversations
I'm convinced that fear prevents us from major breakthroughs in our lives. Many times, it's a fear of having a tough conversation with a staff member that keeps managers from having breakthroughs in their own success.

The most common tough conversations are serious and difficult. For example, you might find a staff member asking for something that isn't perceived by the manager as reasonable and yet, it's hard to say "no." Perhaps the staff member might need to be admonished for something that was done inappropriately but you don't want the person to stop liking you as a friend. Another example might be when a staff member requires a performance improvement plan and conversation about why that's necessary or even the tough conversation of letting someone go. Conversations around reviews, termination, compensation, promotions, and poor performance are all realities of life for every manager.

The best managers don't turn a blind eye. The best managers do not ignore the conversations that must take place. While there is not a rush to have the conversations, and there has been proper thought given to what must be said and how it must be communicated, there is no benefit to succumb to the temptation to procrastinate. To do so is not good management. Many times, it's a lack of understanding about how and what will be said that adds to the fear, and the fear of an unknown reaction.

The best way to approach the discussion is to think about how you would like to be treated if you had not measured up to the organization's expectations. You would like to be treated with thoughtfulness, would like to be listened to, and you would like your manager to understand why and how the situation unfolded. Sometimes it is a matter of not fitting into the culture or expectations of the organization. If that is the case, helping the staff member to find a gracious way to exit the organization is what excellent leaders do. Those leaders are respected for being fair, but firm.

When these conversations are completed, especially after proper preparation and an acknowledgement that no matter the outcome it is appropriate and necessary, there is generally relief. There is a feeling of confidence that while the conversation was hard, it was necessary. And very often, managers will find that the negative person or the situation was an anchor around the legs of the manager and now that weight has been lifted and removed.

When the Great Recession hit, Danny knew that it would be necessary to let many members of his team go. The

CEO mandated cuts across every team and the net loss were 5 FTEs in the Development Department. The decision about the five staff members that needed to be let go was not as difficult as you might imagine. What was difficult was summoning the courage to have the conversation. In advance, Danny wrote out the scripts for each of the five conversations and practiced them. Danny also thought carefully about the potential questions he might be asked and the reactions he might expect that would require a careful response. In scheduling the face-to-face meetings, he thought carefully about the best time and location to have the discussion that would also minimize the awkwardness for the recipients and the remaining staff. In the end, there was a release of internal stress following the conversations. Looking back several years later, Danny knew that event helped him become more comfortable pushing through discomfort. Danny was clear that he intended to help those terminated to find a new position and that he would be a reference for each of them. He also immediately communicated with all the remaining staff that they too were to help those who had lost their jobs and he asked them to help them locate a new position if they were able to do so. Looking back several years later, two of those that had been let go returned to the team and the three others moved on to new jobs and new opportunities shortly after.

"You gain strength, courage and confidence by every experience in which you really stop to look fear in the face. You are able to say to yourself, 'I have lived through this horror. I can take the next thing that comes along.' You must do the thing you think you cannot do." - Eleanor Roosevelt

THE FIVE TOOL FUNDRAISER

Part III

THE TRUSTED CEO AND EXECUTIVE TEAM PARTNER

The Trusted CEO and Executive Team Partner

Over breakfast one day, I was having a great conversation with a colleague and friend about the misconceptions of most nonprofit executives about the role of the fundraiser. Few would acknowledge the many complex dimensions of the professional development officer role while most would point to revenue generation almost exclusively as the expectation.

In all the decades of fundraising, I have rarely read a job description for a Chief Development Officer that speaks comprehensively to the role and expectations of the position. Let me give you a perfect example. In how many position descriptions for a head fundraiser have you seen the expectation listed that they will manage the Chief Executive Officer related to fundraising activities and solicitations? I'm willing to bet that you've never seen this.

And yet, the best fundraisers in the business are every day expected to support, lift up, write for, guide, direct, counsel, and advise, take a bullet for, and generally manage the fundraising expectations of the executive's work. And because you don't see this in job descriptions, and because executives don't like to speak about the lack of experience, expertise, and/or strength they lack in fundraising, the work of the fundraiser in this regard is little written about and hidden from the public.

Even though the role of the development professional related to the CEO, or as an executive team manager, is not well documented or discussed, it is a vital part of the fundraiser's role. It's not just the CEO, or Executive Director, or Foundation President, I'm also talking about key executives that perform significant duties and have extraordinary responsibilities like the Chief Operating Officer, Chief Financial Officer, Chief Strategy Officer, Chief Marketing Officer, or any number of other titles that make up the executive Cabinet.

When the management of this individual or team exists and functions properly, the success that can be generated is quite extraordinary. When the superpowers of a dynamic and capable executive leader are combined with the strategy and expertise of a development professional, transformational philanthropy is the typical result.

In thinking about the unique and important role of the CEO as the fundraiser and as trusted executive team partner, it's also important to acknowledge that many nonprofit executives fail to understand that they are in two very different businesses. I'm here speaking about the primary business of mission delivery, the reason they probably got into nonprofit management. But they are also in a separate business called the fundraising business.

Helping the executive team understand this duality and that each requires a different framework for management and level of investment for success is extremely important for both sides of the business to thrive. Failure to acknowledge this reality has led to more than a few organizational failures and has left money on the table, mission impact limited, and potential constricted.

Our Five Tool Fundraiser consultant father and husband frequently shared an anecdote about one of his former clients, a CEO of a large hospital, who used to say, "Give me more money and I'll give you more mission". Unfortunately, the punchline of the story is that the CEO didn't understand the best practices associated with generating those dollars philanthropically. It was a journey over many years that ultimately led the CEO to hire the right people, make the proper investment in philanthropy, and shoulder much of the burden of cultivating and stewarding donors. The board while also advocating for an exciting vision for the future of the hospital recognized through the leadership of the CEO and the fundraising executive that they could only secure the hospital's future by personally engaging in extraordinary generosity and by assisting the fundraising process in all ways possible.

On the following pages, we take a deep dive into the areas that are particularly important to the fundraiser in the management of an executive or executive team. Each of the qualities and characteristics help secure the fundraiser's role as a trusted advisor and a more successful development professional.

Teacher and Mentor
It is surprising, as many of you have already experienced, the degree of assumptions about fundraising made by people not involved in it on a day-to-day basis. One of the false assumptions I hear frequently is that we just need to reach out to MacKenzie Scott (it was Oprah Winfrey or Bill Gates at one point) for a gift. Another false assumption is that if the organization could just hire the top fundraiser at Harvard, then we would have no problems whatsoever. These assumptions are laughable to those of us in this fundraising business but thought to be so wise by many of the CEOs and executives in the nonprofit world.

We, as development professionals, are in a unique position to counter these false assumptions and reinforce the correct methods of perceiving development. One of the ways we educate is to provide reports. We must provide reports that accurately measure the performance of the Development Office and the individuals involved in it. We can also educate our executives by providing philanthropic data from credible sources within our industries or more broadly with national data. We can also educate by providing white papers on key topics and coordinating strategic conversations with executives that are aspirant peers to provide encouragement and support on a particular topic.

An area of particular importance when it comes to providing education and awareness is around the CEO or executive's responsibilities when it comes to the cultivation and/or solicitation of prospective donors and the recruitment and staffing of key board members. The success of the fundraiser in gaining greater engagement in the fundraising process from an executive is perhaps one the most important ingredients to strengthening the organization's capacity to secure philanthropic support in the short and long term.

Joanne came into fundraising from education. She was a high school teacher before she shifted careers in her thirties to become a development professional. Her teaching background has been a huge help to her in training staff and volunteers in their fundraising roles. However, educating her CEO proved to be extremely difficult because the CEO was not interested in learning or developing the fundraising knowledge nor the needed fundraising muscle. Joanne routinely provided lists of individuals to the CEO that required a stronger connection with the top leadership. Joanne provided white papers and videos on the importance of the CEO as a fundraiser for a nonprofit. After many unsuccessful efforts to engage the

CEO, Joanne found a key advocate and ambassador for fundraising in the Board Chair, who had prior fundraising experience with another non-profit organization. Together, the two of them were able to break through and get the CEO to take small actions by mentoring him to take steps at first and then larger steps later in supporting the fundraising process. Over the years, the trio of Board Chair, Joanne, and CEO created a strong fundraising team and elevated the organization's philanthropic endeavors to new heights.

"I never teach my pupils. I only attempt to provide the conditions in which they can learn." — Albert Einstein

<u>Senior Member of the Leadership Team</u>
The Five Tool Fundraiser is a trusted advisor to the CEO and the executive team. As such, it's common for the best development professionals to be a formal member of the leadership team, Cabinet of the CEO or executive team, and to formally and informally be consulted on all manner of organizational issues.

As a senior member of the organization's leadership team, the development professional has a strong platform to advocate for ethical and mission-focused decision-making, as well as for fundraising. The development professional has an opportunity to explain and teach development, to strengthen the mission and story, to help the organization focus on a vision for the future. The development professional's role might also be to inspire the leadership to seize the opportunity for potential impact the organization can achieve. It's also common for the top fundraiser in an organization to be consulted on a one-on-one basis and in larger groups on major strategic issues given the wisdom and good judgement the development professional is known to possess.

The CEO would describe the Five Tool Fundraiser as wise and trustworthy. This individual is true to their word. When they promise something, they deliver. They achieve their goals – both those that are more individual in nature and then those that are the aggregate goals of the team.

Commonly, the best fundraisers serve as therapists. Few people truly appreciate how lonely it can be for a CEO or executive inside a nonprofit. It can also be lonely for a fundraiser. You often have few people you can truly open up to without fear of backlash. You can't often share with other staff, your board members, or your donors. But because of development professional's wisdom and because of their trustworthiness, executives will often approach the best fundraisers with the most intimate details of their lives and share some of their deepest fears because they have a level of trust that these conversations will remain confidential and a belief that the fundraiser will offer actionable, appropriate, and effective guidance.

Ray and his CEO met every week for an hour and the agenda was always carefully prepared to cover the key elements of the development enterprise that required the CEO's attention. These meetings often went way over the allotted 60 minutes. Ray never booked another meeting directly after the meeting with his CEO. The agenda for the meeting was formulaic though the content was always dynamic. Ray started the agenda by asking the CEO for his agenda items. The agenda then noted key updates from the previous week and quickly migrated to top priorities for the week ahead. They reviewed the CEO's prospect portfolio and made calls and sent emails in the moment, and generally tied up any loose ends. Then came the moment on the agenda for the CEO to bring forward any sensitive or urgent issues. This part of the agenda might take 5 minutes, or it might take 50 minutes. There was no way to prepare for what might come up. However, it was during these discussions where Ray shined. The CEO brought forward all sorts of challenges and issues, both personal and professional, and Ray was always prepared with understanding and wisdom to help the CEO work through even the most sensitive issues. The CEO soon found that his meetings with Ray were so helpful that he began to drop by Ray's office to invite him to go for a walk where they could discuss issues in private. The CEO wanted Ray's thoughtfulness and advice. Ray and the CEO bonded over their walking time together, which became a weekly, unscheduled, time that they both looked forward to.

"All great leaders choose great advisors, people they really trust for their governance." -Tom Payne

Develops Tools and Resources

The great fundraisers aren't just talking heads. They don't merely give guidance and advice. They don't just offer strategy. They are also in the trenches and on the front lines with the staff and executives in creating the content that they and their executives need.

The best fundraisers are developing best-in-class tools and resources and the list of tools and resources that a great fundraiser will create is too long to list. Some of my personal favorite documents that a Five Tool Fundraiser will create, personally or in collaboration with others, includes the case for support narrative, proposals, research profiles, frequently asked questions documents, scripts, letters, strategy briefings, presentations, agendas, training materials, pipeline reports, and so much more.

Often the great fundraisers will identify the tool or resource that the executive or development team needs, provide the opportunity for the appropriate staff member to develop the first draft, and will then review that document to make sure it covers all the bases. Other times, the great fundraiser will recognize the importance of generating some tools, recognize that the expertise doesn't exist within the organization to complete the job, and will find and outsource that task to other professionals.

It's important to understand that the head of development can't do everything. They constantly need to pick and choose the activities that can be done by them, prioritize those tasks that must be completed urgently, delegate work that can be done effectively by others, but always checking to be sure the work meets the highest standards of quality that a shop of excellence strives to meet.

Diana loves to promote the excellence of her organization. She knows her CEO is a rockstar and should have a stronger voice and greater reach nationally on key healthcare issues. Recognizing the opportunity, Diana began working to get the CEO out on the speaking circuit to raise her public profile. This in turn raised the profile of the organization. Additionally, Diana engaged a communications firm to turn the white papers that Diana had ghost written for the CEO into engaging media files that could be used through social media and with key audiences. Interestingly, donors appreciated receiving these pieces as well and were impressed with the CEO's thought leadership nationally on key healthcare issues of the day.

"Behind every great leader, at the base of every great tale

of success, you will find an indispensable circle of trusted advisors, mentors, and colleagues." -Unknown

Facilitates Significant Fundraising Activity and Results
The great development professionals are activators. Some might call them multipliers. They have a way of getting people, in this case executives, volunteers and staff, to do things they would not otherwise do. And in this way, they can leverage the availability and talent of others to contribute to philanthropic revenue.

It takes a special type of person that can get people to be fundraisers. Let's admit it. Many executives are not aware, prepared, equipped, willing, available, coachable, or positive when it comes to fundraising. Most nonprofit executives didn't come up from the development world so it's no surprise it's a bit foreign or uncomfortable. On the other hand, some executives think they know all about fundraising, even though their experience with major gift work is limited. This can be equally challenging and vexing for many fundraisers.

Most nonprofit executives come into their roles with very little experience in fundraising. Some have been connected to the programs of the organization while others come from a for-profit background. Neither of these previous roles adequately prepares the executive for the fundraising expectations of the position.

The fundraising expectations of many executive roles are frequently minimized in job descriptions or in the recruitment process so you're often not able to work with strong fundraisers because they haven't necessarily hired for the right characteristics to learn the development role and do well.

I assume many hiring committees fear that placing an emphasis on fundraising might scare too many good candidates away. Still other organizations still haven't embraced the executive as a key to successful development and don't expect them to lead or engage in this realm. For the head of religious institutions this is very common but it's still a reality in other sectors of the nonprofit space as well.

This can obviously present challenges when trying to recruit a solid development chief who understands the difficulty ahead of not having an executive that supports and understands the fundraising efforts of the organization. I would certainly be asking probing questions about the role of the executive in fundraising if I was serious about a job and would look elsewhere if I was told the executive didn't participate.

No matter where the executive or executive team is in their fundraising journey, the effective executive manager is capable of meeting the leader where they are and convincing them to participate at some level in the fundraising process and will, over time, provide training, coaching, support, encouragement, and more in such a way that they are able to help the executive to productively support the fundraising process for the benefit of the mission and impact of the organization.

Jorge and the CEO of the museum started on the same day. Jorge came to the CDO role from another museum where he was the number two in the development office of a much larger museum. This is his first role as the leader of a development shop, and he was very excited to demonstrate his leadership capabilities. The new CEO of the museum was formerly the CFO of the museum for a few years and had never seen the previous museum CEO engage in fundraising. As far as the new CEO was concerned, fundraising was not an expectation of the role. The board certainly never brought that up when interviewing the CEO nor was it built into the compensation package.

When Jorge realized that the new CEO wasn't in alignment with him about fundraising roles, he knew he had his work cut out for him, but he followed a three-part strategy. Knowing that the new CEO was open to building a network, the first step Jorge took was to connect his CEO with four museum CEOs that he knew were heavily involved in the fundraising efforts of the organization. Jorge next worked strategically with the Board Chair and other members of the board of directors to help them understand the value of having the CEO participate in fundraising and how it would be valuable to have them encourage the CEO to step into this role and learn as much as possible from Jorge and others. Lastly, Jorge was sure to invite the CEO into specific donor meetings where he was confident the CEO could also add value and where success was almost assured. By carefully planning this meeting, there were plenty of opportunities to prepare, brief, and debrief with the CEO before and after the meetings which provided a terrific opportunity to educate and encourage the CEO, and proved to be extremely beneficial.

"Instead of trying to change your boss, focus on trying to better utilize his or her knowledge and skills in service of the work you're leading." – Liz Wiseman

Prepares Executives for Meetings
Executives are asked to participate in all varieties of activities connected to fundraising. The most typical

way executives participate is in meetings with donors and prospective donors whether these meetings are to cultivate, to solicit, or to steward.

Importantly, the best fundraisers prepare their executive for these meetings by positioning the executive for success. Preparation takes many forms. A few of the more common examples of preparation work includes making sure the executive knows the meeting is on the calendar and preparing briefing memos that provide research, outline the executive's role, and share talking points. One of the extra steps the fundraiser might take is to meet in advance of the meeting to role play or walk through key details to make certain there is a level of understanding and comfort before it's too late to make changes that are deemed to be important according to the executive, who might have thoughts to add.

Fundraisers also prepare their executives for other engagements related to fundraising and mission advancement and this includes ghost writing. Writing speeches and providing talking points for group presentations and board meetings are common expectations of the fundraiser.

Frequently, fundraisers are asked to help executives prepare for activities that aren't even directly connected to development. The best fundraisers will craft white papers, letters, agendas, and so many more tools and resources. This is part of the trusted advisor relationship between the fundraiser and the executive. The best fundraisers are often known to be thought partners with their executive.

Stella finds that her executive needs her most often when leading up to and then during the gala. Stella routinely writes the executive's remarks for the event and strategically identifies the individuals who will be seated with the executive during the event. For those individuals at the executive's table, Stella will create thumbnail profiles, and in some cases, full profiles so the executive has a wealth of background information that will help the executive relate to and develop a stronger relationship with these key donors and prospective donors around the table. During the event itself, Stella is frequently at the side of the executive, making sure the executive knows the names of key individuals as they are about to shake hands and enter a conversation. Stella is indispensable to the executive and is a big part of why the executive is seen as thoughtful, engaged, and such a strong relationship builder.

"The purpose of information is not knowledge. It is being able to take the right action." -Peter Drucker

<u>Sensitive and Supportive of the CEO Role</u>
Fundraisers often claim they have the most difficult job imaginable. It's true. The job of the head fundraiser is tough. They are asked to do and deliver so much. Know who else is asked to do and deliver so much? The nonprofit CEO! Like the head fundraiser, the chief executive of most nonprofits is called upon to manage all sorts of complicated relationships, sticky situations and over deliver on expectations of board members, staff, donors, and more.

In this way, the CEO and CDO are connected by a unique bond. They are often in the trenches together like a pair of soldiers. Naturally, the relationships between the pair can become very close and sometimes co-dependent. This is one of the few situations where you probably won't criticize co-dependency, but rather will celebrate it.

The best fundraisers can foster a close and mutually beneficial relationship with the CEO. The development professional uniquely understands the areas the CEO needs support, and the CEO in turn, effectively understands the role of development and how best to support the development function. This is the type of productive relationship that can and should exist.

Importantly, the Five Tool Fundraiser is sensitive and supportive of the CEO's role. They embrace their own responsibilities while also embracing the need to help the CEO navigate the complexities of their own role while helping them succeed in it. In this way, the best fundraisers frequently serve the executive as coach, therapist, administrative support, muse, confidant, best friend, and all manner of things in between.

Darnell never imagined that his Executive Director would come to him for advice. Darnell didn't see it as his responsibility early in his tenure with the nonprofit to be a guide or counselor to the ED. That changed when Darnell was brought into the executive's inner circle and was asked to help with a particularly sensitive issue that involved another senior member of the staff who was being accused of embezzling funds from the nonprofit. The circumstances required a high level of confidentiality, discretion, and wisdom as the executive navigated the situation with the executive committee of the board, lawyers, accountants, and law enforcement. During this difficult time, Darnell proved himself an invaluable thought partner and friend to help the executive navigate these very difficult waters. Darnell offered to prepare a public relations plan and a plan for donor communications should the situation become known outside of the organization. Coming out of that situation, Darnell had proven himself to be trusted and wise and the executive continued to return to Darnell when sensitive issues emerged.

"It is not enough for a professional to be right: An advisor's job is to be helpful. -David H. Maister

Supports the Board Relations Functions

One of the vital areas of fundraising production and greatest sources of the organization's culture of philanthropy emanates from the Board of Directors. Frequently, however, chief development officers are limited in their capacity to influence the identification, recruitment, onboarding, staffing and support of future, current and former board members.

The strongest fundraisers, however, will have a very connected role to the board. They understand that the CEO's boss is the board and therefore the CEO will need board members who will support and work hard on behalf of that executive to help them succeed. Further, the best fundraisers will alleviate the CEO from the burden of managing key board functions for a few reasons. First, the fundraiser has skills in volunteer management that often the CEO doesn't possess. And, secondly, the fundraiser understands that a board needs to be actively engaged, inspired, and guided to properly produce the philanthropic impact the organization requires.

The fundraiser's support of the board functions can take many forms. A few of the more critical areas where the fundraiser can be helpful including the following:

1) Identifying characteristics most effective in terms of

board membership.
2) Reviewing and updating the board expectations document.
3) Preparing and updating board onboarding materials and designing appropriate onboarding experiences
4) Identifying board prospects.
5) Maintaining the board's recruitment pipeline and facilitating the process of the Board Nominating Committee in fulfilling the board recruitment role.
6) Developing the methods of evaluating board impact and effectiveness.
7) Regularly communicating with board members in an effort to help them undertake and complete their roles more productively which might include individual annual work plans.
8) Encouraging and inviting each and every board member to participate financially to advance the mission to the best of each board member's capacity.

Many of these critical aspects of board and volunteer management are explored in greater depth in the chapter that covers the fundraiser's effective support of volunteers.

Ann has seen an increase in engagement of the board since being named Secretary to the Board. In this role, Ann has taken over several key functions related to the management of the board nominating process and board engagement. Ann was given permission by the CEO to be the designated staff liaison for the Board Nominating Committee and that gives Ann the capacity to help nominate the right board members, vet those candidates, and connect the CEO to those future leaders at the right strategic moments. Ann was also able to convince the CEO to allow her to serve as the identified liaison to the board in the fulfillment of their duties. This has given Ann the capacity to follow up with board members directly when there are action items that need to be urgently completed. In this way, the board itself has become more philanthropically focused and many of the administrative headaches that existed for the CEO before are now eliminated.

"No one is more cherished in this world than someone who lightens the burden of another." – Joseph Addison

THE FIVE TOOL FUNDRAISER

Part IV

THE EFFECTIVE
VOLUNTEER
MANAGER

The Effective Volunteer Manager

The effective manager of board and volunteers describes the development professional who can capably identify, recruit, and engage people in the mission of the organization and get volunteers to do things such as fundraising that they would never normally do on their own. The best fundraisers provide a volunteer support system to board members and other volunteers who rely on the fundraiser to help them succeed in their vital roles.

Volunteers are precious. They expand our reach as they introduce the organization, the fundraisers and staff to new people and volunteers who have the capacity to help us with the fundraising process in extraordinary ways.

Many wrongly assume that volunteers are needed to ask for money. While there is certainly value in volunteers who have the desire, willingness, and capability to be an effective solicitor, and follow through on these traits, and actually ask, and secure funds, it's not a necessity for volunteers to engage in fundraising in this way to be valuable to the fundraising process.

There are so many crucial elements to effective fundraising, and they can all be supported by volunteer leadership. For example, volunteers can host events that bring new people who can be potential supporters to the organization. Our history is filled with board members and other donors who initially found an organization through an invitation from a friend. Volunteers can invite contacts to special events whether they are galas, groundbreaking events, or program activities like graduations or educational opportunities. Volunteers can thank donors by making calls or sending notes. Volunteers can help identify and recruit other volunteers. Volunteers can be strong advocates, respected voices in the community who can encourage others to get involved. Volunteers can guide and advise staff on how best to move forward strategically with approaches to corporations, foundations, individuals, member groups, and more.

As you can see, there are more than a few ways a volunteer can help with fundraising, and I only scratched the surface with the dozens of ways.

There are just not enough hours in the day for us to get in front of and make a meaningful pitch to all the great prospects and donors that we wish to engage. Volunteers expand our reach and provide the capacity for us to magnify our reach and impact. They increase our bandwidth and accomplish tasks that we either can't do because of our lack of access or can't do because the cost of hiring someone to do the work would be too prohibitively expensive.

As a result, the best fundraisers command an army of generalists and specialist fundraising volunteers that provide vital support. To understand how these individuals are so effective at identifying, building, and sustaining these effective partnerships, let's dig into several of the key individual traits.

Adequate Orientation and Clear Expectations
It's not uncommon for board members to be recruited onto a board without much understanding of the expectations of their role. Some board members, even after a year of being on a board, will admit that they don't know the programs of the organization, don't have a strong sense of the financials of the organization, and aren't completely

sure what they are expected to personally give each year and/or raise from others.

Providing clarity for board members and other volunteers about expectations is something great fundraisers know how to do. It starts with the recruitment process. Great fundraisers are prepared with vetted and approved board expectations documents that clearly outline what board members need to do when they step into the role. They also provide this document and review the expectations with prospective board members in advance and receive a commitment in writing that these expectations are understood and would be honored if the individual becomes an approved board member.

Traditionally, the board's expectations document is a one-pager and covers key activities like the give-get amount (the amount that an individual board member is asked to personally contribute and the amount that a board member is expected to personally raise), board attendance, committee engagement, no conflicts of interest, prioritization of this organization at a top 3 charitable priority, preparation in advance of board meeting and participation in board meetings, serving as an ambassador and advocate, and more.

Once the board member has been approved, there is meant to be a significant and substantial onboarding process, so the volunteer has a broad and comprehensive overview of the organization's mission, vision, values and knows the programs and people as well as the financials and other aspects that are vital to undertaking the board responsibilities. Well-run organizations will traditionally provide an orientation binder (Welcome to the Board) that is complete with all the essentials to get a board member started. Some organizations now provide these materials digitally, either on a flash drive or accessible through a board member's own log in on the website. Both are terrific, but I personally also love the printed and personalized binder for each board member. It really shows a higher level of care, detail, and significance. And it's harder to ignore.

The onboarding binder isn't sufficient on its own. Most great fundraisers will also schedule a series of meetings for the new board members with key members of the executive team, development team, and program team. There is also an effort to give the new board members several experiences that connect them with the mission of the organization to really drive home the significance of the organization's work. Throughout all these meetings and experiences is the opportunity for the board member to ask questions and develop relationships that will help the board member feel more connected, comfortable, and invested.

The orientation and onboarding of a new board member is not meant to be a one and done event. The process should continue for a six to twelve-month period and should include tactics beyond those already discussed. One of the activities is the assignment of a board mentor or navigator. This would be an individual on the board that has more tenure on the board but would be a great fit with the new board member and someone the new board member would respect and with whom the new board member would appreciate spending time. The other recommended activity is the assignment of a staff liaison assigned specifically to the new board member. This would be a high-level staffer who is one of the key executives for whom the board member can contact any time with questions, concerns, or support.

Ray is on the board of a local nonprofit. From his personal experience, he now understands how frustrating it is for board members to come into a board role and not be told what needs to be done, how to be most helpful, and who to contact with questions and for information. This experience caused Ray to evaluate all board recruitment and onboarding activities for his own organization where Ray serves as Chief Development Officer. Discovering some of the same bad patterns, specifically the lack of clarity around expectations and support during the onboarding process, Ray developed stronger systems for onboarding. From Ray's board experience, he also became aware that new board members have the most excitement about being engaged. Ray now looks for ways to seize the opportunity to engage the new board member early on, instead of waiting until they have had a year or so to learn the ropes. Now, all new board members more clearly understand what they are expected to do and are trained and supported appropriately so these board members can more effectively fulfill their important volunteer roles.

"When people are financially invested, they want a return. When people are emotionally invested, they want to contribute." - Simon Sinek

Ongoing Training and Education

We need to constantly remind ourselves that board members and volunteers don't know what they're supposed to be doing. They don't go to school to learn how to be a fundraiser. They need to be taught and educated.

Through the recruitment and onboarding process, board members and other volunteers can generally learn quite a bit. But the training and education opportunities connected to fundraising must not stop with onboarding.

Every board meeting is an opportunity to learn something helpful around fundraising. Telling can be effective but showing can really help. Old school role-playing, even though some might consider it "hokey", can really make an impression. There was a time when role-playing was expected and respected. Providing real examples of how other board members performed fundraising duties successfully can also be incredibly effective. The modeling and leadership of other board members is vital and highlighting the good fundraising work of board members inspires board colleagues to act. And the Five Tool Fundraiser is competent in sharing those examples and recognizing the good work of their volunteers publicly.

As it relates to education and training, the Five Tool Fundraiser creates tools and a toolbox for their board members and volunteers. Within the toolbox, volunteers can access the things they need to do their assigned jobs. The vital tools are likely to include scripts for setting a meeting, scripts for making an ask, a list of volunteer engagement opportunities, a list of sponsorship opportunities, sample letters, sample proposals, ways to give, promotional materials about the organization or programs, personalized lists of prospective donors to manage, a calendar of key upcoming activities, contract information of the assigned fundraiser and so much more.

As it relates to scripting, I've always found that it's necessary for fundraisers to help volunteers understand how they can use suggested words and create their own comfortable language. Not everyone is in the same place when approaching fundraising and not everyone is willing to do the same things. Some volunteers will end up serving in all types of roles while others may continue to serve in more limited fashions. As the effective development professional, you have the responsibility to help each volunteer reach their full potential as volunteer fundraisers. This requires quite a bit of one-on-one support and significant personalization.

A volunteer's confidence grows substantially when they are well prepared. This typically includes having talking points and a briefing memo that includes details about the meeting time, place, desired outcomes, and information about who will be in the meeting. These resources might not make every volunteer successful, but they assure every volunteer has been given the best chance to succeed and that's really all you can do.

Another effective way to provide training and education is to debrief with a volunteer after a meeting. During this debrief, when you review notes from the conversation and map out next steps, you can also test how things felt for the volunteer. You can say, for example, "Thank you. You did a great job. How did that go for you?" Following their response, you can also ask, "Do you have any thoughts about what you want to do next time?" These types of leading questions can help arrive at learning and improvements in approach in next meetings without having to be overly critical about the volunteer's performance. As a learning experience, you can also point out examples of how you approached "the ask" with the prospect. For instance, you might have said, "Would it be alright with you if I send you some options in writing that you might like to consider? We can then meet again in a couple of weeks to discuss what is of interest to you."

Sarah finds that preparation for a meeting is just as important as the meeting itself. Sarah routinely schedules time before a prospect meeting with the volunteer who will join her. During that briefing meeting with the volunteer, Sarah will review the memo that she has sent the volunteer a few days ahead. The memo includes specifics about the meetings including the key objectives, background information on the prospective donor, and an overview of the architecture of the meeting that also includes suggested talking points, and potential questions that might be asked. Everything is mapped out in advance to impress the prospective donor with the merits of the organization and proposal but also with the preparation that went into the meeting. Sarah also built into the preparation materials, several questions that the volunteer could ask the prospect, which encouraged the prospective donor to talk about why she likes the organization and why she is involved and interested in the programs and services. Sarah knows that you don't often get the chance for a redo in this business so you had better make the visit the best it can be on the first go around.

"By failing to prepare, you are preparing to fail." -Benjamin Franklin

Work Plans and Appropriate Staffing to Accomplish Goals
Not surprisingly, planning the work and working the plan is a helpful strategy when it comes to managing volunteers. Collaborating with your volunteers to create individual and tailored annual work plans is something Five Tool Fundraisers regularly incorporate into their volunteer management activities.

Chris vividly remembers the new member orientation as

a board member for the AFP Foundation for Philanthropy when the Executive Director asked each new board member to develop a work plan for the year. It was the first time Chris had been introduced to the work plan concept and the first time Chris had given any serious thought to the type of activities and impact he would provide as a board member. It caused Chris to realize that without putting thought and intentionality into a plan, Chris wouldn't undertake board responsibilities with any priority or focus.

Because of this planning process, Chris came up with the plan to generate at least $50,000 to establish a permanently named fund in honor his mom, Claudia Looney, to support ethics in fundraising. This was over and above the other expectations of his board role. As a result, Chris became more passionately engaged in the organization, felt a greater connection to its work, and felt like he was truly generating impact and doing something important. Significantly, the organization raised over $100,000 for the fund and secured support from hundreds of new donors in the process. The Claudia A. Looney Fund for Ethics in Fundraising still exists at AFP. We encourage you all to support it!

From that point forward, Chris became an advocate of annual work plans for board members, campaign committee members, and other key volunteers. Included in the traditional work plan for board members are goals around attendance, giving, fundraising, individuals to approach or connect to the organization, committee membership, leadership roles to pursue, special projects, and more.

Importantly, the work plan should attempt to maximize

the utilization of the unique assets that the member brings to the organization. Ask yourself the following questions when working with volunteers?

1. What can be focused on that would be rewarding for the volunteer?
2. What are their specific interests, and can their activities be matched against those?
3. What special talents or skills does the volunteer possess where the organization could benefit?
4. Is the board member, for example, passionate about a particular program?
5. Do they love volunteering their time?
6. Are they extremely connected to others with giving capacity?
7. Do they have specialized expertise in the areas of legal, real estate, construction, accounting, fundraising, or some other industry that can be helpful?

Designing a plan that resonates with a volunteer's interests and expertise can be a real confidence builder and engagement magnet. They will begin to feel so good about their role, proud and satisfied with their work, and willing and able to share positively their experiences with others.

We all know that a plan on its own isn't the solution. You as the fundraiser will always need to support and staff volunteers to assure their proper implementation of plans. The good news is that the plans will provide the proper direction and inform strategy and activities. That will give you as the fundraiser a lot to discuss when you check in with the board members. The challenge is that it takes significant time, energy, consistency, persistence, and organization to manage this process with not one, but many board members. In the end, the accountability and support you provide to these board members will be a huge payoff in the end.

Norman didn't like the fact that the organization entered each new fiscal year without a strong sense of what the board was committed to give and raise. It certainly made it more difficult to build out budgets. It wasn't until the topic was discussed as a board that it was broadly understood that some level of visibility around the probable impact of board giving and fundraising was necessary. Norman received approval to survey each board member about their intentions for the year. This started the culture of board accountability and emphasis on individual and collective board impact that has permeated the organization and allowed the executive team to enter each new fiscal year with assurances that twenty percent of the organization's budget was secure. Baby steps led to bigger and bigger steps and now the organization feels like it's sprinting into the future.

"If you don't know where you are going, you'll end up someplace else." — Yogi Berra

Measures Performance

Peter Drucker is credited with the much-used phrase, "What gets measured gets managed". My father changed the saying. He would say, "What gets measured gets movement." The meaning is essentially the same no matter which way you say it. If you expect results, you're going to need to set goals and provide accountability to that goal by evaluating, or measuring, the accomplishments and progress toward reaching that goal.

Among the individual board members and the board, I love the concept of measuring collective impact and sharing those findings back with the board. Historically, for example, you can share with the board how much the group contributed individually and collectively. You can also share how much the group was able to secure through their own influence. How much in soft credits historically did this group generate? Put those numbers together and you can provide a strong sense of the collective impact on fundraising from the board, both in real dollar terms but also as a percentage of the contributed dollars and the impact on the overall budget. How did the board perform last year in comparison to the five or ten-year history? What is the goal next year in relation to the five or ten-year history? These measurements of performance are hugely helpful in driving the right focus and the right activity.

People, not just board members, are notorious for paying less attention to tasks they find difficult and for which there are few to no consequences for failing to do them. When it comes to board members specifically, the tasks are a bit scary, often require a bit of risk-taking that comes with the potential of rejection, and all this takes time from their busy schedules. Time is not something many of these individuals feel they have a lot to offer and feel like it is among their most valuable asset. Is it any surprise that fundraisers are often frustrated by the lack of activity and progress of volunteers on tasks that they themselves have committed to complete?

The best fundraisers aren't always successful because of luck. They understand human nature and design systems that will increase the likelihood of improved performance both among staff and volunteers. For volunteers specifically, the best fundraisers are often more inclined to micromanage tasks. The great fundraisers take copious notes of the activities that a volunteer commits to complete, follows up those meetings with memos that carefully outline tasks and timelines, and then they actively follow up, checking back frequently on progress on a mutually agreed upon schedule.

The concept of a report card for board members was developed specifically to provide accountability for the responsibilities of board members and to provide a mechanism to evaluate their effectiveness. The best report cards are the ones that provide quantitative and qualitative analysis against those specific expectations that are communicated to each board member. Ideally, the work plans developed at the top of each year provide an additional layer of goals upon which to measure the effectiveness of board members.

With report cards, which are very successful in motivating action among volunteers, there must be a commitment to follow through on the part of the development professional to complete the report card but also confirm the review meeting with the board member. Importantly, successful volunteer measurement will never be truly effective if it doesn't also involve the CEO and/or the Board Chair or some other high-level board member to lead the conversation. While some board members will respect the fundraiser's role and understand that it is a necessary part of their job to evaluate fairly each board member's contribution, many board members will take offense at this dynamic. For this reason, there is a need to put key respected volunteers between you and the board members to keep you safe from pushback and to demonstrate that this is truly an organizational priority that deserves the individual board members full and complete attention.

Anisha runs a fundraising program each year in a small to medium-market city and the Fundraising Chair has been in the same role for six years. For the first three years, this volunteer chair was very active and found a way to lead the effort to raise more money than the year before. In the fourth year, however, the revenue declined. In year five, revenue again declined. Despite the goals being well established, the goals were missed because the accountability functions, including the ongoing measurements of progress, were not strong. As a result, Anisha engaged her CEO to join her on quick monthly check in meetings with the chair. Additionally, every two weeks, a full report was generated on progress against goals. These reports showed where the performance should be according to the plan, where progress was at this same point in previous years and provided very specific strategies and recommended next steps for the following year. As a result, the board raised more and more money each of the following years.

"If you are building a culture where honest expectations are communicated and peer accountability is the norm, then the group will address poor performance and attitudes." -Henry Cloud

Makes Fundraising Fun
No one ever said things that are hard to do in life must also be painful or miserable. Unfortunately, though, the hard things in life are often associated with pain and misery because they don't often come with a facilitator or teacher that can help make them bearable and even fun.

In this way, the best fundraisers make fundraising fun, which is typically challenging under the best of circumstances and filled with frequent rejection, enjoyable. Fundraisers don't eliminate the rejection, though they do know how to take steps to increase the likelihood of success. They don't make fundraising less time consuming, instead they help streamline the process and eliminate unnecessary actions.

The best fundraisers know how to incorporate elements that put the "fun" into fundraising for volunteers and staff. Some of those tactics include things small and large like:

1) Breaking down big tasks into many smaller actions. How do you eat an elephant? One bite at a time.
2) Adding entertainment. Almost anything is more fun with music, dancing, themes, or decorations. Creating a different environment can be inspiring and motivating.
3) Creating a competition. Many times, it is way more interesting and engaging if you add a bit of competition to the role. Turning on the competitive juices among volunteers can move them into action.
4) Provide incentives. What's in it for me? The classic question should be evaluated before asking any volunteer or staff to do anything. Can you as a fundraiser provide some prize or other incentive to the completion of a task or by winning some competition?
5) Do it as partners. Done the right way, partnering around tasks can provide a sense of companionship and accomplishment. Best yet, do it with friends.

These five techniques are just a start to the many ways fundraisers make fundraising fun. As you can see, fundraisers go the extra mile. They don't ever say, "That's outside my scope." If there is something that needs to be done, even if it's not listed among the expected roles of the position, the best of the best will find a way to get the job done well.

In that way, the fundraiser creates a winning team. No one likes losing, and no one wants to be on a losing team. Perhaps this explains why the Yankees are so popular, as an evening outside the city of New York. The Yankees have a history of winning. They have a culture of excellence. And they are also competitive and always have a chance to be victorious. This is the type of aura that the fundraiser desires to create.

Darren knew that many board members felt overwhelmed by the size of the fundraising give/get. In conversations with the concerned board members, Darren was able to chunk out the goals to create more bite-sized milestones that would ultimately build up toward the achievement of the larger goal. Additionally, Darren found creative ways to publicly celebrate and honor those board members that had taken important steps forward toward their goals. As time passed, most board members realized that a step at a time was the solution rather than taking one big jump. Additionally, the work wasn't hard and was rather enjoyable when they were able to do it with Darren who helped to make it easier and a lot of fun.

"Fun is one of the most important - and underrated - ingredients in any successful venture. If you're not having fun, then it's probably time to call it quits and try something else." - Richard Branson

Regular Meetings, Communication and Dialogue

The Five Tool Fundraiser understands how to respect a volunteer and board member's time and make certain that they are using it wisely. We all know that our own time is extremely valuable and understand that volunteers feel the same about their own. Additionally, the Five Tool Fundraiser recognizes that a volunteer's time, especially for those individuals that are major gift donors themselves and help connect and influence other major gifts, is the most important gift they can give us (the organization). The time, talent, and treasure are all connected. If we don't use all these gifts given to us by volunteers wisely, we run the risk of them not giving more to us the next time. When we value and utilize these gifts with discretion and impact, volunteers are more likely to reward us with these gifts again in the future.

To assure that we are being great stewards of a donor's resources, especially time, most Five Tool Fundraisers will create a pattern of regular meetings, communications, and focused dialogue with their volunteers. It's in these moments of communication and connection that the relationship is cemented. The fundraiser learns from the volunteer the type of work that is most rewarding, the time available to commit to the organization's work, the methods of communication that work best, the pet peeves to avoid, and so much more. Now, the relationship also matures in those moments when the fundraiser and the volunteer are in the trenches doing work together, but the ongoing communication assures that the volunteer doesn't feel neglected, lacking support, and without a partner to turn to for answers or help when needed.

We as fundraisers need to be great communicators and to tell stories to our volunteers, so these volunteers have stories of their own to share about the organization with their own contacts. Storytelling is one of the most effective and powerful tools we have. It's our great honor and privilege in our meetings with volunteers to be able to share those key mission moments, client success stories, and other fascinating aspects of our organization that will no doubt help volunteers inspire new contacts to learn more and get engaged.

Janice has a standing meeting with the members of the executive committee of the board. Every two weeks they connect via Zoom to review elements of the individual board member's work plan and to get updates on key elements of the organization's progress. There is always an agenda. On that agenda, there is always one item that is never missed. There is also another item not on the agenda that is never missed. The agenda item that is never missed is a story of a recent client win that the fundraiser hopes will inspire the volunteer, leave an impression, and hopefully be a story that the volunteer can share with others. The item not on the agenda that is never missed is the fundraiser's efforts to confirm that everything is good with the volunteer. The typical question Janice asks at the top of the meeting is, "Everything good with you and your family?" The typical question Janice asks at the end of the meeting is, "Thanks again for your time today. Is there anything I can do to be helpful to you?" The care and concern are real and so too is the feeling of a strong partnership.

"When the trust account is high, communication is easy, instant, and effective." -Stephen R. Covey

Caring and Thoughtful Relationship-Builder
A Five Tool Fundraiser whom I know often tells a great

story of a board member that was personally capable of giving an eight and nine figure gift and though historically generous to the hospital, this board member had never given a gift at that multi-million-dollar level.

Importantly, this same individual had also never asked anyone else, especially her friends and contacts, to support the hospital. She told the fundraiser, "I'm not a fundraiser. And I can't ask my friends. They will stop returning my calls if I ask them to give to the hospital. I will never be able to do that."

This was the board member's position at the very beginning of the hospital's campaign and when the fundraiser had first arrived in the role of Chief Development Officer. Over the course of a ten-year relationship, the fundraiser became a good friend and advisor, trained the board member in fundraising, and gave her baby steps to get her moving in the right direction. The fundraiser joined her in all the campaign work, gave her tools, examples, and models to show her how fundraising could be done successfully and without risk. The board member changed her tune.

After ten years of effort, and the hundreds of lunches and conversations that came with a large campaign, the board member became a willing volunteer who was able to effectively invite others to be a part of the mission of the organization – thereby expanding the financial capacity and reach of the organization. Additionally, this same board fundraising volunteer also saw greater value in the organization and developed a stronger connection and belief in the mission. As a result, this board member was invited to and agreed to give the largest gift to the campaign and the largest gift to the hospital in its history, naming the new patient tower that was being built. The board member's commitment also pushed the campaign fundraising total over goal.

This story is meant to share the importance of the fundraiser as a successful relationship builder and someone that understands the need to meet a volunteer where they are in their fundraising journey. By listening carefully to this board member's concerns and supporting their volunteer fundraising tasks, the fundraiser found ways to unlock their capacity as a significant donor to the campaign and became a fundraising leader in the process. It's not a one-size fits all strategy to undertake with volunteers. Developing relationships successfully requires a customized approach, embracing the unique characteristics and personalities of your volunteers.

Jerry knows that board meetings don't often present opportunities for board members to get to know each other or for Jerry to get to know the individual board members. As a result, Jerry routinely schedules social gatherings for board members that provide unique and fun experiences and bonding opportunities. In addition, he makes it a goal of the annual board retreat to dedicate time to team-building exercises as well as social time. To help Jerry get to know each board member better, Jerry commits to taking each board member out to at least one lunch every year and schedules a coffee date once or twice a year on top of that. Additionally, Jerry connects via email and phone calls on a regular schedule. Managing these required contacts and meetings certainly takes time, but Jerry has the system built so that nothing falls through the cracks.

"I believe that you can get everything in life you want if you will just help enough other people get what they want."-Zig Ziglar

Organizes and Runs Effective Meetings

The Five Tool Fundraiser runs effective meetings. People recognize and appreciate the thought and attention to detail that go into meetings run by successful development professionals. They have an agenda. They have a purpose. There are people in charge, and those individuals who have roles to play in the meeting know the timing, the topic, and deliver the information or discussion items well.

We believe organizing and running effective meetings requires that the following five elements exist. They are inspiration, information, decision, next steps and fun. Let's explore them each in greater detail.

Inspiration - Board members and volunteers respond to inspiration. They want and need to be inspired. You as a fundraiser can accomplish this by providing a mission moment. For some organizations this might be a client testimonial like the student that received a scholarship providing an overview of how the money supported their academic success. Or it might be a doctor sharing the advancements of the research funded by the organization. The stories shared are opportunities for board members and volunteers to learn more and to be reminded why they are so passionate and care so much about your organization.

Information – Fundraisers recognize that board members and volunteers need to leave a meeting with new information that they didn't have before. Importantly, the information that you want to share shouldn't be information they could have found by reading something sent to them in advance of the meeting. Rather, information gained during meetings can be learned from an expert in a particular field like fundraising or finance. The learning might be from a program officer from within your organization. Or perhaps the head of your finance department or head of human resources that shares perspectives and ideas about issues being confronted by the organization.

Decision – What's the point of having a meeting if there isn't an opportunity to provide advice and guidance? Additionally, great meetings provide an opportunity to decide something. The decision doesn't have to be weighty. Decisions can come in all shapes and sizes. Ideally, however, the board, a committee, or a volunteer group can spend time in dialogue, discussing the topic, and feeling empowered to decide about that issue. Obviously, you don't put forward topics that aren't ready to be discussed. But for those issues that are ready, giving the board or volunteer group a platform to talk through the issues will accomplish so much. It will allow them to know their thoughts and ideas are needed. It will demonstrate that their engagement is important. Board members and volunteers, after all, didn't go to a meeting to hear one person talk at them the whole time.

Next Steps – Meetings are wasteful when they don't provide opportunities for board members and volunteers to take next steps on assigned tasks. The meeting itself needs to create ways to engage the volunteer in an activity that can be worked on and/or completed during the time between the current meeting and the next time the group will meet. Creating assignments, or homework, during meetings, assures movement. The development professional organizes the meeting to bring forward assignments, and when those tasks are assigned, the fundraiser is adept at recording, sharing out to the group, and maintaining accountability through follow up. Often that accountability happens with report outs at the next scheduled meeting.

Fun – Meetings should be enjoyable. Meetings are enjoyable when the volunteer learns something new, meets someone interesting, such as a new board member, and/or learns something exciting about the organization's mission and goals that they did not know. It is also fun to feel valued as a volunteer leader. Making certain that the volunteer feels valued will make the meeting an enjoyable experience and will encourage the volunteer to make the next meeting a priority.

Based on notes Ava has taken during the meeting, she starts working on the draft agenda for the next board meeting immediately following the current board meeting. It's the perfect time to understand the gaps in the board's education, where decisions might need to be made, the type of inspiration that could be provided next time, and what is likely to keep the group engaged. Following the board meeting, Ava follows up with the volunteers to ask if they need assistance with the tasks that they were assigned at the meeting. She reminds them that they will be reporting out at the next meeting as it is already on the agenda. Ava plans to have a brief section that recognizes and highlights all the valuable contributions made by individual board members from the last meeting until the current one.

"If there are differences of views or divergence of ideas, they can be resolved through discussion and dialogue." -Azim Premji

<u>Gives Credit and Praise Freely</u>

The best fundraisers look for, finds, and takes advantage of opportunities to celebrate the accomplishments of others.

More than merely thanking volunteers and staff for their good work, great fundraisers go to great lengths to give credit to others. The Five Tool Fundraiser doesn't "hog the limelight." The Five Tool Fundraiser brings zero ego to the table. Even if the fundraiser plays a lead role in some aspect of the fundraising process, they will lift and promote the other individual or individuals involved in the activity or process and position them as the key ingredient to that success.

We must be good at thanking our volunteers and staff to be good at our job as fundraisers. We just can't thank our volunteers or staff enough. Thanking them publicly is great. Thanking them in newsletters or with personal notes is also tremendously effective.

As an example, singing the praises of a volunteer at a board meeting for their fundraising success and sharing that success in front of their peers, will begin process to lead other board members to understand and model the behavior that they are seeing among their peers. They hear about what others are doing. It's peer and pure gold. During these moments, the volunteer feels appreciated and will likely continue the positive engagement pattern. Other volunteers will be educated and inspired to do more. It's a win-win.

Davis worked for a manager early in his fundraising career that always attempted to make themselves look good at the expense of others. When a big gift was secured, for example, this manager took all the credit and refused to acknowledge the important contributions of the staff and volunteers who worked hard to put the organization in the right position to be successful. Recognizing how corrosive it was for managers to have a need to receive praise and credit and then to minimize others to exalt oneself, Davis took active measures to approach leadership differently. Davis has been very thoughtful about giving others credit as often as possible while also trying to be personally humble. Contrary to popular belief, the strategy of recognizing others and taking a back seat has proven to be extraordinarily effective. It is, in fact, a hallmark of his leadership and core to the perception Davis has developed among his staff and volunteers as a servant leader.

"In the best, the friendliest and simplest relations flattery or praise is necessary, just as grease is necessary to keep wheels turning." -Leo Tolstoy, War and Peace

Builds a Culture of Philanthropy
People throw around the phrase, "culture of philanthropy," without a firm understanding of its definition. Most fundraisers and most people in the nonprofit sector have never seen an organization with a strong and successful culture of philanthropy. It's unfortunately rare and quite elusive, and even harder to sustain over long periods of time.

I have traditionally defined culture of philanthropy in the following way. The nonprofit culture of philanthropy describes an organization – from the very top executive, its board and volunteers, and staff members - that believes in and embraces the power of philanthropy to advance the organization's mission. Further, an organization that has a culture of philanthropy puts into daily practice those elements known to be effective in philanthropy, which includes extending personal and broad-based invitations to support the organization financially, engagement in the fundraising process by volunteers and staff alike, caring deeply for donors by showing gratitude and stewarding the relationships well, and supporting the people and systems that allow fundraising success to be sustained well into the future.

The best fundraisers not only know what it means for an organization to have a culture of philanthropy, but they know how to build it as well. It's not easy to build a culture of philanthropy. It takes alignment and commitment to create and grow the culture of philanthropy from organizational leadership – both executive and board – and this is not always feasible given the unique personalities and backgrounds and motivations of some leaders. Building a culture of philanthropy also requires systems and people that are working collaboratively, consistently, and effectively. The best fundraisers know how to fix what's broken and fuel what is working well.

One of the big challenges to arriving at a culture of philanthropy is that it is a destination that requires substantial time to arrive at. Will the fundraising be in their position long enough to achieve the change that is required? The best fundraisers give the time and tenure to the organization to make it possible. The other challenge is that what has been built provides no guarantees that the culture will be sustained without proper constant attention and support. Like a sandcastle that someone labors to build, it will be quickly blown away or trampled without someone taking the steps to protect it from the elements.

Joanna spent ten years at a higher education institution as Vice President for Advancement. During that time, her accomplishments were many. Building a strong culture of philanthropy was one of the biggest achievements. She built a strong board, created institutes for some of the university's key programs. Each institute had its own unique advisory boards, branded cases for support, and staffing that led to strong philanthropic success across a few campaigns. Joanna also developed a strong partnership with the President that resulted in an incredible portfolio of existing and prospective donors that began to support the University in extraordinary and exciting ways. Joanna left the university after a decade to move into the consulting world. Fifteen years later, Joanna was excited to get a call from the current Vice President for Advancement of the same university Joanna had served. It had been a dream for Joanna since leaving to return to the university to help it as a consultant with a future campaign. However, Joanna was heartbroken to learn that all the significant gains she had helped create in philanthropy had been lost. A new President came into the organization that didn't appreciate philanthropy in the same way. The VP for Advancement position had seen tremendous turnover. Board members were no longer held to strong giving and fundraising expectations. The staff had been decimated and the fundraising results were a fraction of what they were a decade prior. Joanna saw painfully firsthand that having a culture of philanthropy is delicate and fragile and should not ever be taken for granted.

"In business, we say that people overestimate what you can do in a year and underestimate what you can do in a decade. This is true in philanthropy as well." -Marc Benioff

THE FIVE TOOL FUNDRAISER

Part V

THE THOUGHT LEADER AND STRATEGIST

The Thought Leader and Strategist

You might have the sense already from reading through all the previous tools of the successful development professional that there are tangible skills and intangible skills involved. When it comes to being a thought leader and strategist, the need for tangible and intangible skills is even more pronounced.

The thought leader and effective strategist speaks to the development professional that thinks ahead, charts an appropriate course, anticipates challenges, and navigates around them, brings people along with them, makes good choices, and finds success whether it's smooth sailing or a bumpy ride.

One of the biggest issues preventing many from achieving their full potential as a thought leader and strategist is time. We are all the victims of "busy-ness". We need more time to get things done on our task list. The most successful Five Tool Fundraisers, though it's hard for most people to see, have more on their task list, get more done with their time, and still want more time in their day to be even more effective. These individuals have a sixth gear that many other development professionals don't possess.

Not having time, however, does not excuse poor planning or a lack of proper execution. The Five Tool Fundraiser doesn't make excuses. They make it happen. Successful development professionals are somehow able to get a tremendous amount of work done, knocking tasks off their list, while also spending time thinking ahead.

Importantly, it's more than just time management and time prioritization that allows the opportunity for thinking and strategizing. It's the commitment to find the time and space to strategize and plan.

Additionally, spending time on strategy and planning does not guarantee a positive outcome. The outcome of the Five Tool Fundraiser's time devoted to thinking and planning is often inspired. This is perhaps where the intangible qualities of the Five Tool Fundraiser come into play.

I'm so impressed by the Five Tool Fundraiser in the way they are so competent in completing tasks while also being able to see into the future, anticipate trends and possible outcomes, not be blindsided, bring everyone along with them, and architect and navigate the proper future.

On the following pages, the thought leader and effective strategist is explored in greater detail. Like me, I believe you will find that this tool might be among the most challenging to develop as a professional and might be the most elusive. It's still incredibly important to the success of the development professional and cannot be ignored or sacrificed.

Always Looking Ahead

Great fundraisers are so busy thinking about the hundreds of things that must get done in a single day. The strategist and thought leader is also taking the long view, spending time and energy charting out a course for the organization, helping it plan for the future. An effective strategist and thought leader never fails to look ahead.

The ability to plan and successfully chart a course requires the great fundraiser to anticipate challenges while also anticipating opportunities. I liken the skill to a strong chess player who can see the entire board, looks at not just the next move but the next two, three, four and five moves ahead. Interestingly, it's not just the chess player's own moves that are considered. The chess player must also evaluate the opponent's moves, anticipated and actual moves, which will determine the eventual course of the game. There are always multiple scenarios to consider, and the effective strategist is aware of them and not surprised nor caught off guard when the landscape shifts and changes.

It's exciting when an individual leader is so strategic that you can tell that they have a decision tree mapped out in their head. As a result, they can tell you right away that choosing one path will result in a negative consequence and choosing the other provides the greatest opportunity for success. While the effective strategist is not always 100 percent accurate, and no human in fundraising ever is, the strategist and thought leader that can look ahead is more often right than wrong and inspires confidence in others to be followed.

Jesse relies on technology to help him remember, prioritize, and manage the dozens of new tasks that come his way every day. Some of these tasks require immediate attention while others can be tackled in future weeks, months, or years. Jesse uses another project management program that resembles a GANTT chart that covers every element of his work from staff management, systems, fundraising goals, board recruitment, special event fundraising, grant management, and more. Importantly, the action items that are tracked on this project management program emphasize and have more detail with the 30-, 60-, and 90-day work but there are also details connected with the 6- and 12-month action items to lest he or other members of the team, allow something to fall through the cracks. The third big program that Jesse uses is his prospect pipeline report out of the database which focuses Jesse on the work he must do in connection with prospective donors and prospective board members over the next 30, 60, and 90 days. Jesse's ability to identify the key tasks that must be accomplished down the road and translate that into tracking systems has kept Jesse from feeling too overwhelmed and preventing him from feeling out of control.

"The duty of planning the morrow's work is today's duty..." - C.S. Lewis, *The Screwtape Letters*

Takes Initiative
We all know that waiting for the phone to ring isn't an effective strategy in fundraising. That's not how to raise money. Fundraisers are proactive individuals. They make things happen through activity. They throw a lot of spaghetti on the wall and some of it will stick.

In the same way, the effective strategist and thought leader doesn't wait. They don't sit around and dream, "That's someone else's job. I don't need to do it." The best fundraisers take the initiative. They don't wait to be asked. They seize upon opportunities. They drive things forward. They make things happen. They are change agents.

I'm specifically speaking here to those issues that are connected to mission advancement but aren't necessarily fundraising specific. Crisis management issues are one example of where an effective strategist and thought leader will often take the initiative. When an emergency arises, even outside the fundraising realm, the fundraiser is often the one that speaks with wisdom about next steps and offers the action plan for a response.

I'm not advocating for fundraisers to do other people's jobs. We've all struggled with staff that refuse to do their own work because they are lazy, self-absorbed, or incompetent. It's impossible to be the savior in every situation. However, the best fundraisers are unwilling to let the ball drop when the opportunity exists to create a solution, particularly if the crisis is impacting donors and prospects. If it's feasible to help, the best fundraisers will find a way.

I'm also not advocating for fundraisers to put their nose where it doesn't belong. We all need to understand and appreciate boundaries and know where we shouldn't meddle or don't have agency to be involved. But the best fundraisers never strictly stay in their own lane. They add value to the conversation.

As true leaders, strong strategies and thought leaders identify problems that others might not see, come up with solutions that others might not create, and continually strive to create excellence across all aspects of the organization even if this means venturing outside the traditional job description.

The effective strategist is the type of person that you want to have the ball dribbling down the court with 20 seconds left to go and the team is down by two. They create opportunities for the other members of the team to be successful. And, if no one on the team is open for the pass with time about to expire, they will gladly and confidently take the shot themselves for the win.

While Anna was the CDO of a human service organization several years back, she was called into the CEO's office and told confidentially that there had been an accusation of theft made against the CFO by a member of the accounting team. Anna immediately asked, "who else knows?". Anna was the first to be told. Together, they developed a plan that included sharing the accusations with the Board Chair, their attorney, and the police. They collected and preserved evidence. Anna was designated as the point person and even though it had nothing to do with fundraising activities, it was essential that she be given this responsibility. Over the next several months, Anna liaised with authorities, the lawyers, the Board Chair, and the CEO, and eventually, when the CFO was arrested and removed from office, Anna was responsible for dealing with the press, alerting the board, sharing the news with key donors and prospects, and supporting the CEO in dealing with the issues around the finance department. The work Anna did in donor stewardship and public image protection was vital. This was not something Anna could have ever imagined or wanted, but at the end of this long and difficult process, Anna knew that she had done a great service for the organization, and she knew confidently that there wasn't much she couldn't handle after managing this very difficult situation.

"Even if you're on the right track you'll get run over if you just sit there." -Will Rogers

Big Tenter and Seeks the Wisdom of Others

When I talk about people as being, "big tenters," I often get a puzzled look back. I'm not sure who came up with the term but I'm a fan of the concept. It very effectively speaks to one of the amazing talents of great fundraisers. The capacity to bring together large groups of people under one roof, often with competing interests or no interest at all, and get them all to be singing from the same song sheet is a skill the Five Tool Fundraiser has mastered.

There are two general concepts connected with being a big tenter. The first involves getting everyone to the party that needs to be there. The second involves the inclusion of voices that aren't necessarily in total agreement even though it might initially be disruptive. As a result of this big tenter work, we often see the Five Tool Fundraiser as a spark – a catalyst.

In my campaign work, I often used the analogy of a big tent to explain the moment when I thought an organization was ready to make its campaign public. It wasn't about the dollar amount raised. It was more about the percentage of close donors and friends that were included to date.

I would often explain that the organization must be sure that everyone considered part of the organization's family should be introduced to the campaign and invited to participate in the campaign at some level first, before the campaign is taken public. In this way, you make sure that everyone important to the organization is inside the big tent before you launch your campaign publicly. You haven't left friends and family and those that would consider themselves to be closely connected to you on the outside. Once you've successfully made your friends feel engaged and connected and aware and important, you can now begin to extend invitations to those that remain outside the tent that should be invited inside.

The other concept of the big tent relates to the pursuit of wisdom by involving many counselors to create the proper path forward. An effective strategist has mentors, and those mentors are treasured and engaged. They seek advice from those mentors and ask questions. They are life-long learners and are open to the advice and wisdom of others.

Often, the voices invited to provide wisdom aren't in alignment at the outset. Commonly, the best fundraisers are particularly effective in bringing together strong personalities – the CEO, Board Chair, donor, program staff, and others. It's often the role of the fundraiser to work with these disparate groups and individuals to find the middle ground, to find consensus, the broker deals, and to navigate through knotty issues. This is called leadership.

An effective strategist recognizes their own limitations. They don't pretend to know everything. They don't attempt to accomplish everything on their own. They don't move forward by proclamation. When it comes to planning, whether it's developing an organization's strategic plan, or an annual development plan, creating a case for support, or anything important in between, the best fundraisers seek the counsel of their advisors. There is an appreciation that wisdom comes from many counselors, and that if something is planned thoughtfully and with the advice of others, the opportunity exists to develop and implement that initiative more successfully.

Tony appreciates the moments when his organization launches strategic planning initiatives. As the CDO, planning efforts like this provide a unique opportunity to engage a variety of stakeholders. When done properly, the organization can hear from, learn from, and utilize the wisdom of staff, volunteers, community partners, the board, donors, prospective donors, and clients. There are few moments in an organization's life that offer the opportunity to collect the wisdom of so many individuals while also bringing them into the inner circle of the organization.

"Do I not destroy my enemies when I make them my friends?" - Abraham Lincoln

Casts a Big Vision
Like most strong leaders, the best fundraisers can formulate a vision for the future of the organization that inspires people to engage and invest.

The capacity to cast a big vision requires imagination. While the best fundraisers must be realistic, they must be dreamers. They understand that doing more of the same is not the secret to unlocking financial support. The ideas need to be big. They must be "BHAG" ideas. BHAG stands for Big, Hairy, Audacious, Goal(s).

The best fundraisers understand that funders are not merely giving to an organization anymore because of reputation or tradition. Organizations now have too much competition, and they constantly need to be prepared to justify their impact.

Great fundraisers paint a vision for the future that people believe is important and necessary to achieve. Further, the best fundraisers give confidence to donors that the big vision is achievable because the fundraiser and the organization's leadership have the capacity to translate vision into reality with the fuel of proper funding.

The proper vision presented to prospective funders and stakeholders is often the result of substantial assessment and evaluation of the past, present, and future situation. The best fundraisers are uniquely able to interpret the history of the organization, or the cause being supported, and know where the organization and cause fit in the grand scheme of things.

The best fundraisers can evaluate trends and anticipate with clarity where the situation is moving in the future. This provides the capacity to position the organization well for that future. The vision cast by the fundraiser takes all the past, present, and future assessments into consideration so the big vision that results is simple to explain despite the complexities and intricacies that were involved in its development. To have the ability to make the complex simple is one of the amazing attributes of the skilled fundraiser.

Some of the readers might be reading this and have the idea that casting a big vision for the organization is not the provenance of the fundraiser but is more often the responsibility of the chief executive or the Board of Directors. There is absolutely truth to that statement. In many organizations, other leaders do have the responsibility to formulate the vision. And in other situations, the fundraiser doesn't have an agency to participate in this realm. But, when a fundraiser is truly the best, their voice is needed and heard. Their visionary ideas for the organization are considered thoughtfully. Their voice is requested. Their voice is required. And they do not disappoint, bringing life to the idea, providing the language to explain the possibilities and inspire the supporters, or, in many cases, coming up with the vision themselves.

Nancy has never been the creative type. One of the strengths of her leadership comes from her ability to bring the right people to the table in those moments when big decisions need to be made. Nancy is a firm believer that she doesn't need to be the best at everything but needs to be able to have access to the best of everything to be successful. She is a multiplier for sure. And Nancy also knows that a rising tide lifts all boats. When she is successful, so will many others in her organization. When the opportunity arose to work on the organization's vision statement with the President, Nancy felt confident in her understanding the organization's past and the current and future landscape of the work. When combined with the creative talents of her communications consultant, and the practical needs of her program team, Nancy partnered with her executive to create a strong vision for the future of the organization.

"Dreams can become a reality when we possess a vision that is characterized by the willingness to work hard, a desire for excellence, and a belief in our right and our responsibility to be equal members of society." -Janet Jackson

Creates Strategic and Tactical Plans

The best fundraisers have tremendous skill and experience. These talents often give them the capacity in difficult or complex situations to "fly by the seats of their pants" and still come out successfully. It's easy to rely on skill and experience alone. Laziness often leads to shortcuts.

The best fundraisers are the least lazy people I've met. Additionally, they are natural planners and prefer to undertake processes that involve planning when it comes to creating strategic and tactical plans. They enjoy answering questions. They appreciate gaining the advice of stakeholders. They are fascinated with mapping out the steps to get from point A to point B.

There is a difference between strategic plans and tactical plans. Great fundraisers can build them both.

Strategic planning is a process used by organizations to identify goals, the strategies necessary to accomplish those goals, and the internal performance management system used to monitor and evaluate progress. The strategic planning process typically culminates in the development of a strategic plan document that serves as the organization's collective roadmap.

Tactical planning is a process of understanding and documenting the written outline of the specific actions you're going to take to address a problem or achieve a goal. It could list the tasks that you'll do yourself, and the tasks you'll assign to employees.

The two planning processes, strategic planning, and tactical planning are complementary. One is typically more high-level while the other is getting into the weeds. The best fundraisers live in both worlds. They function successfully in the atmosphere, and they thrive on the ground as well.

We often hear about people who have their head in the clouds. This is most frequently not a compliment. However, people with big vision and big ambition often do live in this space. What separates many effective leaders is the capacity to come down off that perch, break down the herculean tasks that many strategic plans or big goals require, and define the step-by-step tactical approach to getting the job done.

As the saying goes, "how do you eat an elephant? One bite at a time."

Within the context of the development department specifically, I find the best strategists have multi-year plans in place. These individuals despise the concept of raising money one year at a time. Instead, they want the bigger picture. They want to see the trends and evaluate the growth potential. They want to be strategic around where to make investments and how to manage staff investments. With that larger perspective, great fundraisers can drill down and create the tactical steps required to achieve the vision.

Adam looked forward to budget season starting in September. The fiscal year for his organization is the calendar year. Every September, the CEO and CFO would ask for the development department budget. It was easy for Adam to provide this because the key numbers and big investments were confirmed the year before and sometimes many years prior. You see, Adam and his team have a three-year development plan that is evergreen. Every year they evaluate the plan goals to make sure they are still relevant and appropriate, and they also add an additional year onto the back end of the plan. This plan, which is socialized with the CEO, CFO, Board of Directors, and other stakeholders, is tweaked as needed. But the existence of the plan itself makes the case for investment stronger and action easier for Adam when it comes time to implement.

"An idiot with a plan can beat a genius without a plan." - Warren Buffet

"If you fail to plan, you are planning to fail." -Benjamin Franklin

Makes the Complex Simple
It's easier to make simple things more complex than it is to make complicated things simple. Being an effective

strategist and thought leader is the ability to make very complex things simple.

There are numerous complexities when it comes to nonprofit organizational issues. Presently, leaders in development face enumerable challenges when it comes to staffing. Work-life balance, the accommodation or consideration of remote or hybrid working environments, the call to be more diverse and inclusive in hiring practices, to pay better, to promote more quickly, to be fair and equitable in all matters related to evaluation of performance, the capacity to retain top talent, shed the weaker performers, all the while maintaining a positive culture, are just a few of the issues that compete for air in the ecosystem of a leader. Despite these staff challenges and complexities, not to mention the other challenges presented by organizational leaders, donors and volunteers, the best fundraisers provide clarity and simplicity.

Most people would speak about a talented fundraiser saying that they know where you stand. The Five Star Fundraiser strategist communicates what needs to be done and does so in a way that is plain and understandable. It starts with listening. Listening is perhaps the first step in comprehension on both sides – the fundraiser and the volunteer. Through comprehension, an effective strategist and thought leader can formulate thinking and narratives that can be generally understood by a variety of audiences.

The effective strategist doesn't speak a language people don't understand. If the work of the nonprofit is scientific or with lots of jargon, the best fundraisers can break it all down and explain it in a way even a fourth grader could understand and yet dress it up so that an adult won't feel like they are being treated like an infant.

If there are 10 or 100 or 1,000 steps that need to be taken to achieve a particular goal, the best fundraisers will be able to communicate to the audience the over-arching aim of the initiative and focus on the next few steps that are essential for moving the project forward. In this way, they simplify the effort and simplify the message, so people don't get paralyzed by fear or paralyzed by not knowing what to do next.

The capacity to unpack, to analyze, to problem solve, to chart a course for the future and be able to communicate it all is what brings people along and has them feeling invested in the outcome. This is an extraordinary talent.

Bernice would never admit this publicly, but the television shows that her children watched were such a valuable training tool in communication. They always teach you to break things down and keep it clear and simple. When thinking about how Bernice works in academic medicine as a fundraiser, perhaps she should be called a translator. She reads research reports, scientific journals, medical journals, meets with high-end researchers and physicians, and then translates this medical alphabet soup and the extreme medical complexities into proposals that donors can understand. She is well-regarded for this talent, the result of which is several $100 million gifts to the university hospital.

"Simple can be harder than complex. You have to work hard to get your thinking clean to make it simple" -Steve Jobs

Inquisitive and Leans In
Asking questions shows interest. Asking questions also

indicates curiosity. The best fundraisers seek knowledge, want to know things, learn things, help solve problems, avoid challenges, become better, or make things better in the future.

These attributes require curiosity, and being inquisitive comes naturally for the Five Tool Fundraiser. An effective strategist proactively seeks understanding. They lean into things that are important and take the initiative to learn in areas that are necessary for the advancement of their knowledge base and the advancement of the mission of their organization.

Leaning into philanthropic understanding is valuable. There are a whole host of areas of philanthropic understanding that require study. Some of the most common areas include artificial intelligence (AI), analytics, macro trends in philanthropy, social media, gift planning, and so much more.

Many of the best fundraisers didn't have previous experience in gift planning or a background in law or finance as they moved up through the ranks of the organization. To acquire knowledge of planned giving, most fundraising leaders have learned on their own. They have read books, attended seminars and webinars, met with estate planning attorneys, talked to colleagues, accessed the toolboxes of experts, and perhaps most important, they have worked with donors on their own gifts to gain practical experience. All the above come second nature to the best fundraisers.

The Five Tool Fundraiser isn't afraid of what they don't know. Rather, they embrace those areas and see the opportunity to grow their own knowledge base. They recognize that they don't know what they don't know and aren't afraid to call upon experts or hire expertise to support those areas that require experience. The best fundraisers aren't apologetic and don't consider it a failure for not knowing something. Like a great explorer, the best fundraisers look forward to moving into the unknown and enjoy the journey toward understanding as much as arriving at the destination of expertise in a particular area.

Early in Jonathan's career, public speaking was challenging. Any time Jonathan was required to give a presentation, he was incredibly nervous, and it wasn't hard for the audience to see his discomfort and anxiety, especially hearing the shakiness in his voice. Jonathan wasn't a naturally shy person, so the fear of public speaking was hard for Jonathan to understand. Fast forward 25 years, Jonathan is one of the strongest public speakers in the country and presents regularly at conferences on a variety of topics including major gifts, engaging boards, and hiring the best people. Jonathan never let his fear stop him from pursuing opportunities to speak. He leaned into his fear and discovered over the years that his nervousness stemmed from his lack of comfort, experience, and knowledge around the topics he was discussing. The more experienced and knowledgeable Jonathan became around a particular topic, the more comfortable he became presenting the information in front of audiences.

"We keep moving forward, opening new doors, and doing new things, because we're curious and curiosity keep leading us down new paths" -Walt Disney

Understands and Anticipates Trends in Philanthropy
The great strategist understands philanthropy. They understand how philanthropy fits into the nonprofit space,

and how it fits into national and global marketplace today and into the future. They have a sense of how philanthropy has evolved and anticipate well how things will continue to evolve into the future.

On a micro level, they understand the motivations of donors and have an acute awareness about the motivations of donors in their sector. They know the profile of their best donors, know what they like, what they expect, and how they want to be asked and stewarded. This allows them to identify and cultivate new prospective donors constantly.

With their own organizations, they analyze data and know the community demographics. These things, among other areas, allow them to better anticipate changes in the community that will affect the organization. This helps them steer the ship toward the proper heading. Too often we see development professionals going back to the same playbook, even if it's tired and not delivering results. It takes courage to take hold of the steering wheel and change direction, especially a new one, but that's common for a Five Tool Fundraiser.

On the macro level, the Five Tool Fundraiser has a breadth of knowledge and awareness of what's going on in the broader world of philanthropy. They can look at a trend such as more dollars being given to charity from a smaller number of donors and formulate measures that will mitigate that or even reverse that trend within their own development enterprise. The best fundraisers know how to adopt the best ideas, thoughts, trends, and practices and put them to practical use for the benefit of their organization's mission.

While the Five Tool Fundraiser has strong instincts when

it comes to making decisions that affect fundraising, I believe the best development professionals don't rely on their instincts alone. Rather, instincts are confirmed by research. Tapping into the expertise of others, digging into the numbers to make metrics-based decisions, and reading the available studies and literature on a particular topic feed into the decision-making process of the Five Tool Fundraiser.

Lara looks forward each year to the release of the Giving USA report. Although the report provides the aggregate national giving date for the previous year, the trends that it highlights and lessons that can be learned are vital and help inform decisions that she makes for the balance of the calendar year and beyond. It's not just Giving USA that Lara finds particularly important. She consumes anything and everything she can related to philanthropic research because she knows it makes her decisions more thoughtful and productive. Lara particularly likes the Bank of American's Report on High-Net-Worth Philanthropy, Fidelity's Giving Report, information provided on the Giving Pledge website, and the daily digest of news provided by Philanthropy.com.

"You have to do the research. If you don't know about something, then you ask the right people who do." -Spike Lee

Corrects Course as Needed

A chef is an individual trained to understand flavors, cooking techniques, create recipes from scratch with fresh ingredients, and have a high level of responsibility within a kitchen. A cook is an individual who follows established recipes to prepare food. The Five Tool Fundraiser is more chef than cook.

The best development professionals don't merely follow instructions or a playbook like a cook does when preparing a meal. The Five Tool Fundraiser understands philanthropy, how to raise money from a variety of fundraising mechanisms, how to build and implement complex fundraising programs, and how to coordinate the efforts of many stakeholders, such as the CEO, the board, volunteers, and the staff.

Additionally, the best fundraisers recognize when a plan is not working, and they will make course corrections as needed to get the organization or its fundraising efforts back on track. Sometimes course corrections are required because the fundraiser made a mistake. Mistakes are inevitable. For the Five Tool Fundraiser, it's not about being right or wrong and they don't believe they are infallible. They admit readily when they have made a mistake and change course to correct the mistake or error.

The Five Tool Fundraiser never thinks of some fundraising activity as perfect. There is always room for improvement. Something done well must indeed be celebrated, but when the revelries are complete, there must be time for reflection and analysis. How can this activity be improved in the future? How can we make improvements to raise more money next time? How can we raise this money more effectively or efficiently next time? These are all questions the Five Tool Fundraiser ask because they are striving for perfection even though they are more than comfortable in the understanding that perfection can never be attained.

David and his team were riding a high from last week's successful gala. The fundraising event, for the 10th straight year, exceeded its goal. Everyone on staff has been saying to David that the event was the best one yet. Even some of the hardest to please board members were overheard saying the same. Despite the accolades, the date of the event post-mortem is set, and David looks forward to meeting with the gala committee and the key members of the development team to review the elements that everyone felt should be repeated and the ways that next year the event could be improved. During the previous year's post-mortem, it was recommended by the committee that the next gala should stay at the same venue, but the master of ceremonies and auctioneer should be upgraded. The other major suggested shift was the placement of the President's remarks near the top of the event before the crowd became too rowdy and too focused on the party. Each of these changes kept things fresh and strengthened the event around the margins without interfering with the successful model they've built over the last decade.

"Mastery is great, but even that is not enough. You have to be able to change course without a bead of sweat, or remorse." — Tom Peters

Maintains Focus on Activities that Raise Money
Shiny objects, personal issues, office drama, and never-ending organizational meetings are all examples of activities that can steal time, energy and focus away from fundraising.

The Five Tool Fundraiser maintains a laser-like focus on the activities that generate revenue. They pick up the phone whenever a donor or prospective donor calls. They will even pause a meeting to attend to the needs of a donor.

They minimize distractions by setting expectations

properly. They also have gatekeepers that understand the priorities and know the approved guidelines of when to interrupt and when to take a message. The Five Tool Fundraiser doesn't do any of this blocking and tackling alone. Like a good quarterback, the offensive line needs to be incredibly strong.

Generally, the Five Tool Fundraiser does the paperwork in the evening to be able to focus on the tasks that move relationships forward during the day. One of the ways great fundraisers can maintain such high levels of productivity is that they offload tasks that don't actually require a Vice President's attention. They also let people do their jobs and if the people they have can't be trusted to independently do their jobs, they work toward finding a replacement.

Importantly, the Five Tool Fundraiser knows acutely that prioritization of limited time resources is essential. The best fundraisers will often pause when doing something and ask themselves, "is this going to help raise money?" If the answer is that the activity doesn't map to money, the Five Tool Fundraiser will often find a way to hand it over to someone, buy time to do it later, or put it on the shelf and return to it at a more appropriate time.

There is a saying in fundraising that meetings raise money. When people say this, they are not referring to internal staff meetings on topics that don't measurably move the fundraising efforts of the team forward. Meetings, in this sense, refer to engagements with volunteers, staff, donors, prospective donors, and other stakeholders that have a real opportunity to move the needle closer to closing gifts.

It's obviously impossible to eliminate organizational and staff meetings that don't support fundraising or those covering non-fundraising topics. No one is immune from these meetings and many of them are arguably very important to the health and well-being of the organization and its people. However, the Five Tool Fundraiser doesn't hide behind these meetings as a reason for unproductivity. They don't seek these types of engagements and volunteer for roles they shouldn't take on because it's easier than fundraising. They avoid these traps and protect their time and energy for the real work of fundraising.

Carolyn finds the most difficult time of the year for her personally is review season. With seven direct reports and a development team of 50, the requirements of preparing for, delivering, and following up on reviews are cumbersome. Carolyn estimates that it's no less than 5 hours of her time per review per senior leader. On top of that it's an equal amount of time to support her senior team with their own reviews. Carolyn cares deeply about the professional satisfaction of her senior members and the entire team. She wants those that have proven themselves to be exceptional members of the team to advance professionally within the organization and she works diligently to seek generous compensation for their efforts as well. The struggle is to maintain a diligent focus on fundraising activities throughout this period. It's not a perfect system by any means but Carolyn has mapped things out exceedingly well and has the support of her administrative team to assure all reviews are completed thoughtfully and completely. She made certain that all reviews happen in person with sufficient time for dialogue and personal connection, including the follow up needed with HR and the employees themselves, and to assure the individual goals, changes to salary and title, and other elements are all managed with precision. Despite the herculean effort Carolyn gives to employee reviews, time for fundraising is never sacrificed.

"Time is what we want most, but what we use worst." -William Penn

<u>Navigates around Politics – Keeps Drama to a Minimum</u>
Maintaining a focus on fundraising is one thing. Navigating around all the intrigues, office politics, and "water cooler" talk is something entirely different.

Have you ever noticed that trouble seems to follow certain people? I'm talking about all the people within an organization. Not just the top leader. So, the question is… does trouble really follow them, or do they create it, crave it, feed off it, or enjoy being a part of it? Either way, the Five Tool Fundraiser will not get caught up in the office drama and will steer clear of those types of unhealthy exchanges that hurt people and suck away precious time that could otherwise be dedicated to fundraising.

The best fundraisers know better than to ignite firestorms. They navigate around those issues. They certainly don't gossip about other members of their team and are incredibly careful about how they describe the successes and failures of other people so that nothing can be misinterpreted. Clear communication and positive communication are essential. The advice that you wouldn't want to say anything, or write anything, that you wouldn't want printed on the cover of the New York Times is so helpful.

The Five Tool Fundraiser is good at neutralizing drama when they see it. They are not afraid to confront those individuals who are creating problems in a private and tactful way. Setting the expectations first, giving a warning the next time, and escalating the issue if it continues the third time is not uncommon. Not addressing the issues condones drama and leaves the team feeling vulnerable and unsafe.

Culturally, the Five Tool Fundraiser builds teams that respect one another and support one another. The team that thrives is the one that lifts each other up and stands there for one another in good times and in bad. This occurs only when the team leader, the Five Tool Fundraiser, is setting the right example and providing strong modeling of the right behavior. And, when there are bad apples in the bunch, "cancers in the clubhouse" to use a baseball term, those individuals are quickly removed and replaced with those that will add value to the positivity and the productivity of the enterprise.

Adam walked into a hornet's nest of dysfunction and negativity on his team when he took the reins a few years ago. It was among the most significant professional challenges of his career, eliminating the gossip, negativity, and backstabbing that he had discovered. In his search for the root cause of the problem, Adam discovered that it was his predecessor and the executive team that modeled poor behavior. One of the first things Adam did was to establish a zero-tolerance policy to eliminate all behaviors that discriminated, harassed, or demeaned others. Adam wanted to be unambiguous and vocal that fundraising is a team sport and there is no success when individuals don't put the team ahead of their own personal interests. Adam worked with the executive team to make sure this same message was cast among all staff across the institution. Over the first 18 months, Adam was able to weed out those individuals on his team who exhibited behaviors contrary to the vision of a supportive and caring culture. Most left on their own accord when they knew that their fire was being starved oxygen. Other troublemakers were let go. Though the process of change was not as quick as Adam would have wanted, the environment was so much better. Adam was able to show that there is fun in fundraising under the right circumstances.

"The supreme quality for leadership is unquestionably integrity. Without it, no real success is possible, no matter whether it is on a section gang, a football field, in an army, or in an office." -Dwight D. Eisenhower

THE JOURNEY IS
THE DESTINATION

The Journey is the Destination

There are Five Tool Fundraisers in this world. We've met them. You've probably met them too. You might be one. They aren't unicorns. There are, in fact, many Hall of Fame fundraisers in this world and we desperately want to create more.

However, there are no perfect fundraisers. Every fundraiser, from those starting out in their first development job, to those that are winding down their career after 50 years, can learn more and have the capacity to do their jobs better every day. We firmly believe in striving to get better every single day. The Five Tool Fundraiser, as you can probably guess, continues to learn and grow every day throughout their career.

The accumulation of experiences adds value to each decision. Five Tool Fundraisers readily share their life-long learning with those they are mentoring or coaching. The accumulation of past experiences enables the best fundraisers to make good decisions. They can identify the unintended consequences of each decision, pursuing options where success is more likely and shunning the pathways where failure dwells. The phrase, "Been there, done that!" is meaningful in fundraising as it is in many professions.

The journey toward becoming a Five Tool Fundraiser is never complete. The journey is the destination. The journey is where fundraisers hone their craft and do things so easily, they become second nature. And when the basics are second nature, the journey toward becoming a Five Tool Fundraiser allows you to develop and perfect some of the more technical skills or specialties in fundraising that truly define the Five Tool Fundraiser.

This entire book has been dedicated to helping the fundraiser find the tools, the skills, the roles, the traits, the characteristics, the actions that will allow you to success as the most well-rounded, competent, and capable fundraiser possible. The five tools we've covered (the effective solicitor, the staff manager, the board and volunteer manager, the executive partner, and the strategist and thought partner) are essential to know, to develop, to sustain if your goal is to be a successful Chief Development Officer, a great fundraiser, and/or a Hall of Fame development professional.

We hope you can use the knowledge gained from this book to enhance your own personal talents. Fair warning, though, you can become less effective, and you can become known as a former Five Tool Fundraiser, someone who used to be great, if you fail to use these lessons over time.

Fundraising skills atrophy and knowledge and skills become outdated in this fundraising business. The best fundraisers stay current, relevant, and practiced. Like a body builder, it takes reps and increasing weight to build muscle. Reps and working through more complex issues will build your fundraising strength.

Unfortunately, no book can give you what you need completely. You will get far more from the on-the-job, practical, real-world fundraising experiences. We hope this book complements these experiences, arming you with knowledge and strategies to consider incorporating that will lead you to greater success.

Through this book, hopefully you have been exposed to

some characteristics and talents you didn't know you needed or didn't know you had. Now that you are perhaps aware of characteristics and talents you need to develop or enhance, will you seek growth? We encourage you to gain experiences in all the Five Tool Fundraiser areas.

The two of us have always felt that mentoring and developing fundraisers, especially the next generation of development leaders, is one of the most important professional responsibilities we have. Please strongly consider who in your orbit might be the type of Five Tool Fundraiser that can be of assistance to you and ask them for their guidance and help.

If through this book we have helped further this profession and have positioned you as well as other fundraisers to become more capable and well-rounded, we will consider this writing exercise to be an incredible success.

As we leave you, please know we wish you all the best in your future fundraising endeavors. Reaching your fullest professional fundraising potential is our sincerest hope.

Please reach out to us and share how this book has helped you. And if there is additional information we can provide, please visit us at www.fivetoolfundraiser.com.

ABOUT THE AUTHOR

Christopher Looney

Chris Looney has committed his professional life to the advancement of the nonprofit sector and remains most interested in elevating the field of philanthropy and the capacity of fundraisers to succeed.

Chris is the son of two legendary fundraisers. His wife, Anisha, works in development as well for a well-known research hospital.

For nearly 25 years, Chris provided advice, guidance and support to hundreds of organizations in his role as a senior leader of for one the nation's largest and most successful fundraising consulting firms. During his tenure with the firm, Chris assisted client partners to raise hundreds of millions of dollars.

Through the years, Chris also served in key leadership positions connected to philanthropy. AFP International Foundation for Philanthropy, AFP of Orange County, The Giving USA Foundation, and Giving Institute have all benefitted from the leadership of Chris Looney.

After decades working on the front lines of fundraising, guiding and advising a multitude of nonprofits on philanthropic initiatives, Chris developed The Five Tool Fundraiser concept.

Over the years, Chris has continued to explore the Five Tool Fundraiser framework, which has resulted in the completion of several books and training materials.

Chris and his wife, Anisha, live in Irvine, California with their three children.

ABOUT THE AUTHOR

Claudia Looney

Claudia Looney, FAHP, ACFRE is the Founder and Principal and Managing Director of Covenant Philanthropic Solutions, a firm she launched in 2008 with her fundraiser husband James Looney. Today, Covenant is a leading fundraising consulting and management firm with partnerships that covers all sectors of the nonprofit industry and major parts of the globe.

Claudia's passion for the world of nonprofit development and management has inspired her to dedicate the past 50 years to helping organizations fulfill their missions. Prior to starting Covenant, Claudia served for more than a dozen years as the Senior Vice President at Children's Hospital Los Angeles where she led and managed all aspects of the fundraising activities and was responsible for overseeing the capital campaign that raised more than $1.3 billion. This was the largest campaign at the time for a freestanding Children's Hospital.

Prior to her tenure at Children's LA, Claudia served as

President of Northwestern Memorial Foundation in Chicago and successfully led the organization's $125 million campaign. As Vice President of Planning and Advancement for the California Institute of the Arts (CalArts), Claudia initiated and completed two campaigns: a $60 million building and endowment campaign and a $20 million emergency earthquake renewal campaign. As President of Saddleback Medical Center Foundation, Claudia began and completed two campaigns, including raising funds to build the Women's Hospital.

Claudia has been recognized for her dedication and service to the fundraising profession in multiple ways. In 2019, the Southern California Association of Healthcare Development awarded Claudia with the Inaugural Legacy Leader Award. In 2012, Claudia was recognized with the Award for Outstanding Fundraising Professional presented by AFP Global. In 2004, Claudia was awarded YWCA's Woman of Distinction for Orange County. Claudia was named 1996 Fundraiser of the Year in Los Angeles and 1994 Fundraiser of the Year in Orange County.

Claudia is past Chair of The Woodmark Group's Board, which oversees the Children's Circle of Care program for the top 25 children's hospitals in North America. She is also past chair of the Association of Fundraising Professionals (AFP) Foundation and was a member of its Global Ethics Committee. Claudia is currently an AFP Orange County board member. She is a Fellow, a past board member, and served as Chair-Elect of the Association for Healthcare Philanthropy (AHP). Claudia is a Certified Fundraising Executive (CFRE) and has published several articles for both AFP and AHP Magazines, including Partnering with the

CEO, Maximizing Physician Fundraising, Donor Relations Redefined, Engaging Volunteers, and more. Most recently, Claudia collaborated with her fundraiser son on a book entitled, The Five Tool Fundraiser.

Claudia received her BA from California State University in Fullerton and is an alumna of the Charter Class of Pitzer College. Her husband, Jim, is a Principal of Covenant. Together, Chris and daughter-in-law, Anisha, also a fundraiser, have blessed Claudia with three grandchildren, and spending time with them is a particular passion.

PRAISE FOR AUTHOR

"A must-read playbook for fundraisers and especially those looking to move from being a Development Director to a Chief Development Officer. Claudia Looney and Chris Looney, the dynamic mother and son duo, provide a step-by-step approach to developing the strategies and skills necessary to excel in fund development, managing up to senior leadership, and connecting with supporters and their teams. Claudia and Chris's words of wisdom in The Five Tool Fundraiser are uniquely illustrated through insightful real-world examples, and compelling storytelling."

- DAWN S. REESE, CFRE, CHIEF EXECUTIVE OFFICER, THE WOODEN FLOOR

"People are central and essential to achieving our mission, and therefore, the retention, development and recruitment of our fundraising team must be a top priority. The timeless principles and real-life examples in The Five Tool Fundraiser will provide you and your team with powerful tools necessary for breakthrough results. The Looney name has been, and continues to be, synonymous with fundraising excellence. I highly recommend this book to anyone who wants to

move their organization to a new level of transformational philanthropy by reaching your fullest professional fundraising potential.

- THOMAS J. MITCHELL, SENIOR ADVISOR TO THE PRESIDENT, UNIVERSITY OF FLORIDA

"The Five Tool Fundraiser is uncommon common sense for the nonprofit sector. It's especially inspirational if you're moving into a leadership fundraising role as a Director of Development, Vice President of Advancement or a Chief Development Officer. Tried-and-true best practices are outlined clearly and enhanced by the most up-to-date techniques, so the book is as valuable for seasoned leaders as it is for fundraisers new to the leadership role. Nonprofit trustees and CEOs will also benefit from learning how the five tools support volunteers and staff presidents alike. Highly recommended to anyone connected to nonprofit fundraising!"

- TOM JACOBSON, PRESIDENT, GREATER LOS ANGELES ZOO ASSOCIATION

"Based on their 80 years of combined fundraising experience, the mother-son team of Claudia and Chris Looney describe the traits they've seen in the most successful fundraisers. Anyone interested in fundraising can learn from these characteristics and the anecdotes they share."

- JETHRO O. MILLER, CHIEF DEVELOPMENT OFFICER, PLANNED PARENTHOOD FEDERATION OF AMERICA

"I have read many books on fundraising and non-profit management throughout my career. The Five Tool Fundraiser is far and away the most accessible and relevant for our time. Whether you are a seasoned fundraising executive, a CEO, or just starting your fundraising career, The Five Tool Fundraiser is an essential primer on how to achieve fundraising mastery. Thank you, Claudia and Chris, for sharing your wisdom with us!"

- J. SPENCER MEDFORD, SENIOR VICE PRESIDENT/CHIEF ADVANCEMENT OFFICER, THE HENRY FORD, DEARBORN, MICHIGAN

"In The Five Tool Fundraiser, Claudia and Christopher Looney, who possess over 50 and 30 years of fundraising experience, respectively, have curated a valuable collection of accessible essays about skills and practices shared by the best philanthropy professionals. For chief development officers, it serves as a stark reminder of what really matters; and, for any fundraiser aspiring to leadership, it is a road map."

- CHARLES L. KATZENMEYER, VICE PRESIDENT, INSTITUTIONAL ADVANCEMENT, FIELD MUSEUM

"Having just read The Five Tool Fundraiser, the book resonated with me. It's a straightforward, engaging description of the most effective ways to practice and lead in philanthropy.

If followed, the reader will be ready to strengthen an organization, build a meaningful career, and accelerate good in their community."

- KENYA M. BECKMANN, CHIEF PHILANTHROPY AND HEALTH EQUITY OFFICER, SOUTH DIVISION, PROVIDENCE

"I'm proud to have known and worked with Claudia and Chris as friends and colleagues the last two decades and have witnessed their dedication to the fundraising profession and non-profit sector. If you want to elevate your career and make a lasting impact on your organization, their book, The Five Tool Fundraiser, is a must-read with a tested and proven framework for you and your team members to achieve greatness in fundraising."

- NICOLE SUYDAM, PRESIDENT & CEO, GOODWILL OF ORANGE COUNTY.

"The Five Tool Fundraiser is a masterful guide that has greatly impacted my understanding of fundraising and philanthropy. Chris and Claudia's work offers a comprehensive and practical exploration of the essential tools required for success in the field of fundraising. The five tools are not only insightful but also presented in a manner that is accessible and engaging to readers of all levels of experience. As a professional in the fundraising sector, I found the emphasis on The Successful Solicitor to be particularly invaluable. Their approach to developing a well-rounded fundraiser that aligns with an organization's mission is both strategic and *pragmatic. This book offers an exceptional resource for those seeking to elevate their fundraising efforts by combining a clear vision with actionable tactics. The Five Tool Fundraiser also excels in its attention to the interpersonal elements of fundraising. Chris and Claudia underscore the importance of cultivating and nurturing relationships with donors, emphasizing trust, empathy, and authenticity. Their insights and recommendations in this regard are not only relatable but also rooted in real-world experience. Moreover, this book stands out for its effective combination of theory and practice. The inclusion of practical examples and real-life scenarios enhances the learning experience, making it a hands-on guide for anyone in the field of fundraising. The writing style is engaging and approachable, making complex concepts easy to grasp. In summary, The Five Tool Fundraiser is a valuable resource that I wholeheartedly recommend to anyone interested in the art and science of fundraising. It provides a comprehensive foundation for success in the philanthropic sector while inspiring a sense of purpose and passion for the work we do. Chris and Claudia's expertise and dedication to the field shine through in this book, making it a must-read for fundraisers and philanthropy professionals alike."*

- JUSTIN COLEMAN, DIRECTOR OF DEVELOPMENT, THE SALVATION ARMY CALIFORNIA SOUTH DIVISION ORANGE COUNTY

BOOKS BY THIS AUTHOR

365 Fundraising Truisms

365 Fundraising Truisms: Daily wisdom for the aspiring Five Tool Fundraiser

There are so many fundraising expressions and many more fundraising truisms that have been passed down through generations of fundraisers and these deserve to be documented and preserved. This book records 365 of the most ubiquitous and relevant truisms in the fundraising field. Give yourself a year, one truism each day, and see how the investment of 5 to 10 minutes elevates your capacity as a five tool fundraiser.

Made in the USA
Middletown, DE
28 September 2023

39411672R00089